As an expert in criminal tactics and personal security methods, Louis R. Mizell, Jr., has made numerous media appearances—including *The New York Times*, *NBC Nightly News with Tom Brokaw*, *The Philadelphia Inquirer*, and a variety of talk shows—to discuss the various ways people can protect themselves.

In *Street Sense for Parents*, he offers specific, up-to-date advice on how to:

* Talk frankly with your child about molesters and abductors
* Protect your child from household accidents
* Reduce your child's risk of being poisoned
* Defend your child against animal attacks
  And more

Children need extra care to ensure their safety. This book will teach you how to protect your child, even in today's dangerous world.

Berkley Books by Louis R. Mizell, Jr.

STREET SENSE FOR WOMEN
STREET SENSE FOR SENIORS
STREET SENSE FOR PARENTS

STREET SENSE FOR PARENTS

Keeping Your Child Safe in a Dangerous World

LOUIS R. MIZELL, JR.

BERKLEY BOOKS, NEW YORK

STREET SENSE FOR PARENTS

A Berkley Book / published by arrangement with
the author

PRINTING HISTORY
Berkley edition / September 1995

ISBN: 0-425-14947-1

BERKLEY®
Berkley Books are published by The Berkley Publishing Group,
200 Madison Avenue, New York, New York 10016.
BERKLEY and the "B" design
are trademarks belonging to Berkley Publishing Corporation.

PRINTED IN THE UNITED STATES OF AMERICA

10 9 8 7 6 5 4 3 2 1

For the Children

Contents

Contents

Acknowledgments

Genuinely concerned about the security and safety of children, more than 300 people from all fifty states and seven different countries contributed their energy, their stories, and their expertise to this book. Police officers, journalists, teachers, researchers, librarians, students, victims, parents of victims, and experts in a dozen different specialties pulled together in a sense of community that seemed almost spiritual. To these people I would like to say thank you. Every one of you has saved a child's life. Although my profession is one of bombs, blood, bullets, and brutality, these people confirmed what I have always believed; most people are caring and good.

A special hug and thank you to Becky Boyd, my administrative assistant, who put her professionalism and love into this book, kept the bureaucracy off my back, and, even at 3:00 A.M., kept cool under pressure. Becky, you are the best of the best.

Wise beyond her years, my friend Maureen Becker made good use of her MBA and cheerfully gave her heart and soul for the children. You are a special and wonderful woman. Thank you.

Trained as an artist and a dancer, Jennifer Barnhard brought style and grace to my office and organized over 300,000 incidents reviewed for this book. Methodical, accurate, and consistent, Jennifer made the machine run smoothly.

John Willig, my friend, partner, and literary agent, led the charge for this book and ordered me to "write something that will help keep my children safe."

The Berkley Publishing Group immediately recognized the importance of *Street Sense for Parents* and said "Do it!" Natalee Rosenstein, Donna Gould, Karen Ravenel, and Aileen Boyle—thank you for standing by me. I appreciate your professionalism and enjoy working with you.

Many friends and associates contributed in their own unique way to this project. I can feel their spirit on every page of this book. It was an honor to work with you. Thank you. Peter Roche, Aura Lippincott, Marie Barnes, Jan LaMarre, Bleu Lawless, Matt Tyszka, Robert Webb, Patrick Friel, Suzanne Conway, Patty Raine, Victoria Brown Barquero, Sheri Mestan, Carol Stricker, Susan Stalick, Karie Newmyer, Betty Baker, Sally Hamilton, Esther Mizell, Dave Fishel, Paige Fishel, Mary Papp, Don Moss, Jim Grady, Don Feeney, Jose Hernandez, Richard Ward, Sean Malinowski, Gary Saylor, Liz Harrington, Chris Leibengood, Tim Dixon, Tony Deibler, Jeff Bozworth, Dave Haas, Steve Fakan, Chris Ferrante, Mike Harrington, Dave Gaier, Bill Penn, Steve Swankowski, Jennifer Mar, Steve Mayes, Grace Goodier, Joan Lombardi, Joe Hemsley, Lisa Hollingworth, Sam Cruce, Jim Hush, Anne Cusick, Rick Watts, Bill Elderbaum, Bill Friedlander, Ed McCarthy, Bill Miller, Joe Mallet, Penny Reid, Jamie Smith, Sara Schoo, Bill Trites, Karen Tamzarian, Joan Andrews, Jim Asher, Dennis Bochantin, Bowman Miller, Ray Baysden, Paul Sorenson, Jim McWhirter, Tonya Matz, Mary Griggs, Jane Garzilli, Allegra Leibengood, Isabelle Claxton, John Gibbons.

Dozens of organizations and associations generously contributed information and expertise "for the children."

I was very impressed with the U.S. Consumer Product Safety Commission located in Bethesda, Maryland. Everyone I talked with provided a gold mine of information and seemed to genuinely "give a damn." Special thanks to Don Switzer, Jacqueline Elder, John Preston, and Warren Mathers.

Rose Ann Soloway and the American Association of Poison Control Centers enthusiastically answered questions and provided data I could not find elsewhere.

Jo Gutierrez of the *Houston Chronicle* and Althea Orvis with the Idaho *Statesman* researched a number of important incidents for this book.

Anyone who loves children should thank ChildHelp USA, the National Center for Missing and Exploited Children, Parents of Murdered Children, the National Victim Center, St. Jude Children's Research Hospital, Mothers Against Drunk Drivers, the Adam Walsh Center, the Polly Klaas Foundation, the Kevin Collins Foundation, and the National Safe Kids Campaign.

Introduction

Nothing is more important to parents than the protection and safety of their children. Nothing! As you read this book you will be listening to the voices of 300,000 young crime and accident victims. You will be learning valuable lessons from their 600,000 mothers and fathers. These children and their parents want to help you. Listen carefully. They are the experts.

Strangers are going to abduct 5,000 children in the United States this year. Hundreds of thousands of children are going to be sexually abused. And over one million children are going to be hurt or killed in an accident. Ninety percent of these crimes and accidents are absolutely preventable.

Children are abducted from every conceivable location: bus stops, schools, shopping malls, and playgrounds. In Boise, Idaho, eleven-year-old Jeralee Underwood was forced into a car while collecting money from the customers on her newspaper route. She was raped, murdered, and dismembered by a man who had previously committed ten rapes, ten robberies, one murder, and four attempted murders. Five-year-old Melissa Brannen was wearing a Sesame Street outfit with a Big Bird emblem on her skirt when she disappeared from a Christmas party at her apartment complex in Lorton, Virginia. A twenty-seven-year-old grounds-keeper, who had attended the party, was convicted of kidnapping with intent to defile, but Melissa has never been found. Ten-year-old Holly Piirainen was visiting her grandparents' home in Sturbridge, Massachusetts, when she and her five-year-old brother decided to stroll down a country road to see a neighbor's litter of puppies. Holly's little brother went home first. But later, when another brother went searching for Holly, all he found was one of her sneakers. Hunters found Holly's body ten weeks later in a heavily wooded area, five miles from where she disappeared. Like hundreds of other murderers, the person who abducted and killed Holly Piirainen is still at large.

The chapter on "Child Abductions" will discuss the tactics strangers use to lure children into vehicles. A child aware of a tactic is less likely to become a victim of that tactic. "Child Abductions" will discuss the tricks, ploys, and deceptive techniques kidnappers use at bus stops, shopping malls, and playgrounds.

Readers will be shocked to learn that in *hundreds* of cases, strangers have slipped into bedrooms and abused or abducted a child as parents slept nearby. Twelve-year-old Polly Klaas was kidnapped from her upstairs bedroom during a slumber party and later murdered. On April 23, 1994, in Vero Beach, Florida, a seven-year-old girl was taken from her bed at midnight, forced out a window, and raped in a nearby park. The forty-four-year-old transient charged with the child's abduction and rape had been arrested in Texas ten years earlier for a similar crime. In that case, he abducted a sleeping ten-year-old girl from her bedroom. On July 2, 1994, in Lodi, California, twelve-year-old Katie Romanek was abducted from her upscale home at knifepoint. The kidnapper, who tied up two other girls in a bedroom, pretended he was interested in buying the house, which had a "For Sale" sign posted outside. Katie was found wandering in a field one day later, wearing only her socks.

The chapter "Child Molesters: Facts About Pedophiles" is designed to educate parents and children about the realities of sexual abuse. Education is our best defense.

Sexual abuse of children is a widespread problem that is occurring in the home, the school, and the religious community. Eighty percent of all sexual crimes against children are committed by a relative or someone the parent and child knows and trusts. While parents are busy guarding against strangers, their children are frequently being fondled by a friend, neighbor, teacher, relative, or member of the clergy.

Irony abounds. In 1993 a judge sentenced an FBI agent, an expert on child abuse, to twenty years in prison. For fourteen years the agent had been sexually abusing his own four daughters. The abuse started when the girls were three years old and continued until they were in high school. In a letter to the court, one daughter wrote: "We have never really had a father. The person who was in the father position wasn't a father to us; he just used us as his play toys."

It gets worse. David Harrington, a private school principal in Maryland, was voted Big Brother of the Year in 1986 and honored by President Reagan at the

White House. The next year he was convicted of having sex with a number of the young boys he met through the Big Brother program. Walter Lee Golden, a planetarium director for a school system in Florida, was voted Jacksonville's Big Brother of the Year in 1981. In 1990 Golden was found guilty of chloroforming and sexually abusing several boys, ages seven to seventeen. He had been using the school board computer to record his seductions. But one of the biggest surprises was announced in 1992 when Eliot Wigginton, a former National Teacher of the Year, and founder of the innovative Foxfire teaching method, was convicted of molesting a ten-year-old boy. In other cases, a Teacher of the Year in Florida, a Father of the Year in New York, and a man who appeared as "McGruff the Crime Dog" at children's parties were all charged with sexually molesting children.

Pedophiles are found in all professions. They have been pediatricians, psychologists, priests, pilots, plumbers, professors, police officers, and photographers. In at least 1,800 cases they have been Boy Scout leaders.

Incredibly, more than one hundred children are known to have been abducted or sexually abused by men and women who had dressed as Santa Claus or as circus clowns. In one case, police arrested a Santa Claus who had molested a five-year-old girl at a shopping mall. Investigators discovered that "Santa" was a wanted felon and had a criminal record for performing sexual acts on the corpse of a young girl. Child molesters dressed as clowns have been arrested in a dozen states. In Washington, D.C., a man dressed as a clown attempted to lure children into his van. A thirty-four-year-old man in Texas who dressed as a clown and made balloon animals for children confessed to murdering two little girls. In Florida a woman dressed as a clown was painting funny faces on children at a shopping mall. The same woman kidnapped a ten-day-old girl and murdered the infant's mother.

This year about 7,200 children, age fourteen and under, will be killed in a wide range of avoidable accidents, 50,000 will be permanently disabled and 13 million will be injured seriously enough to require medical attention.

Firearm accidents kill about 1,500 people a year in the United States, mostly children, and seriously wound thousands of others.

The stories are always the same, year after year. One child finds the "hidden" handgun, another child climbs a chair and grabs the "unreachable" .45, and still another pulls the trigger on what he thinks is a toy gun.

Over and over again we hear, "I didn't know it was loaded," "I forgot to lock up my gun," "I was just cleaning my handgun," and "We were just goofing around."

Most people are surprised to learn that dogs bite 1.5 million infants and older children each year in the United States. Each year a dozen children are killed by dogs, hundreds are horribly mauled, and thousands require hospitalization for less serious bites.

Many dog owners are shocked to learn how expensive a lawsuit can be when their dog bites a child. Recent lawsuits resulting from dog attacks have been settled for $425,000, $800,000, and $2.6 million. One dog owner who claims he was "mauled in the courts" told the author, "When a pack of lawyers catch scent of your money it's worse than a pit bull attack."

Without question, more children are helped by dogs than are hurt. Address the safety issues and dogs are indeed man's best friend.

Drownings are perhaps the most avoidable of all accidents. More than 300 children under the age of seven drown in residential swimming pools each year. Another 2,500 children are treated in hospital emergency rooms for submersion accidents. But swimming pools are not the only danger. Hundreds of children have also drowned in bathtubs and buckets.

On May 9, 1994, in Florida, an eight-month-old girl, left unattended in a bathtub, drowned in four inches of water. The thirty-three-year-old mother had placed her baby in a bath seat and left to answer the phone. The bath seat fell over, dumping the child facedown in the water. In Michigan, on June 2, 1994, a three-year-old boy wandered away from his home and fell into a neighbor's unfenced in-ground swimming pool. After a frantic one-hour search, the boy's father lifted his neighbor's flexible solar panel pool cover and found the lifeless child. On June 30, 1994, a seventeen-year-old baby-sitter in Normandy, Florida, found an eleven-month-old girl caught headfirst in a five-gallon bucket of water that she had been using to clean the apartment.

Representing freedom, independence, and adventure, bicycles, for most of us, are the ultimate symbol of a carefree childhood. With a hot wind blowing in our faces, a bicycle becomes a white stallion, a jet plane, or a race car wheeling us into a whole new world. But a child's dream often becomes a nightmare.

About 500 children are killed each year in bicycle accidents and another 500,000 bicycle-related accidents are treated in hospital emergency rooms.

Children are also killed and injured in household accidents. Some are electrocuted, burned, or scalded. Some are killed or injured from falls or falling furniture. And other children are run over in their driveways or die after ingesting drugs, cleaning solvents, and other poisons. "Household Accidents" identifies the most common and most serious accidents and provides tips on how to save lives.

The greatest danger is the danger you never considered. "The danger of windows never even occurred to me," said the mother of a young boy who broke his neck falling from a town-house window. More than one hundred children are killed each year falling out of windows. Thousands of other children suffer spinal cord and neck injuries, fractured skulls, multiple broken bones, and other serious injuries.

Toys are supposed to be fun, not dangerous. But each year the United States government is forced to recall millions of toys because they are in violation of safety standards.

Many toys have hidden dangers. At least thirty-five children are known to have been killed when the lids of their toy chests slammed down on their delicate necks.

"Dangerous Toys" identifies many toys that have choked, strangled, cut, and poisoned children.

Deadly accidents involving children occur every day and take many different forms. On April 12, 1994, in Plymouth Meeting, Pennsylvania, a three-year-old boy died of asphyxia when a power window in his father's car closed on his neck. On April 20, 1994, in Muskegon, Michigan, a two-year-old boy was killed in his backyard when a discarded 200-pound bathtub leaning against a tree fell on him. The toddler was standing near the tub when his fourteen-year-old brother tried to move it. In Nashville, Tennessee, on June 16, 1994, a two-year-old boy died of heat stroke when he was accidentally left in a van that was supposed to drop him off at a day-care center.

When it comes to safety and security for children, *awareness* of the danger is one of our most effective defenses.

There has probably never been a more violent time in America, a more difficult time to be a parent, or a more dangerous time to be a child.

John F. Kennedy once said, "Our country's most valuable natural resources are our children." *Street Sense for Parents* is designed to save and protect our most valuable natural resources.

1

Child Abductions

The disappearance of a child is every parent's worst nightmare. Approximately 4,600 children are abducted by strangers (nonfamily members) each year in the United States. Most of these boys and girls are sexually abused and traumatized but are soon returned to tearful parents. Sadly, an average of 300 children each year suffer long-term abductions. These 300 children are either murdered, never found, or are returned to their families months or years later. But these statistics don't tell the whole story. There are also about 120,000 attempted abductions each year. The attempted abductions are usually unsuccessful because the targeted child is armed with knowledge, the kidnapper cannot isolate the child, or because an adult knowingly or unknowingly interrupts the would-be kidnapper's scheme. It is, of course, good news that so many abductions are averted each year. The disturbing news is that 125,000 of our children this year will be targeted for abduction by a wide range of criminals.

Children have been abducted from bus stops, schools, shopping malls, carnivals, and movies. They have been lured away from playgrounds, parks, swimming pools, and video arcades. And perhaps most frightening, children are increasingly being abducted from their own bedrooms while parents sleep nearby.

It is not enough to just tell our children, "Don't talk to strangers." We need to be a lot more specific by explaining that there are some bad people in this world and the tactics these bad people might use. A child aware of a criminal tactic is less likely to become a victim of that tactic. Education is our best weapon.

Children Abducted From the Home

Petaluma, California, is a quaint rural town surrounded by ranches and dust-colored hills. But on October 1, 1993, an incident in this small, sleepy town sounded a wake-up call that aroused parents nationwide.

At 10:35 P.M., twelve-year-old Polly Hannah Klaas was kidnapped from a slumber party in her upstairs bedroom, as her mother and six-year-old sister slept in another room. Polly, a brown-eyed girl with shoulder-length brown hair, was playing a board game with two girlfriends when a bearded, bushy-haired man entered through an unlocked door, crept upstairs, and barged into her bedroom. Armed with a long knife, the man told the frightened young girls to lie on the floor and to be quiet or he would slit their throats. As he bound and gagged the girls and put pillowcases over their heads, he asked which of the girls lived in the home. When Polly spoke up, the intruder demanded to know where the money and jewelry was hidden. But instead of taking the valuables that were pointed out, the stranger stole Polly, a pretty and precious jewel more valuable than any possession. He picked up the slender, eighty-pound child, ordered her friends to count to one thousand, and carried the whimpering seventh-grader into the night. The girls freed themselves about twenty minutes later and woke Polly's mother, who called the police.

The body of Polly Klaas was discovered December 4, 1993, on the grounds of an abandoned lumber mill, thirty miles from her home. The little girl who dreamed of becoming an actress had been strangled to death.

Most parents believe that criminals will avoid a residence if someone is home. Wishful thinking! During 1994 alone, criminals entered over 500,000 homes and apartments while at least one family member was present.

The Polly Klaas case was not unique. In recent years strangers have come out of the night and sexually assaulted, kidnapped, or killed hundreds of America's children, girls and boys, in their own bedrooms. Cases of home invaders attacking young children in their bedrooms have been reported in almost every state.

But not all the victims of this bizarre and brazen new trend have been murdered; there are other scenarios. Some of the victims have been sexually abused in their own beds by intruders who then threaten to kill the child if he or she tells anyone about the incident. Others have been abducted from their bedrooms, abused a short distance away, and then allowed to return.

Known as the "child molester who stalked America," David Lee Thompson, a forty-one-year-old truck driver,

traveled the interstates and abused young girls ages
three to eight in Massachusetts, Illinois, Indiana, Missouri, and several other states. The monster in every
little girl's dream, the bogeyman beneath every boy's
bed, Thompson would stalk his prey by day and creep
through their windows at night.

Stopping his truck in small towns, Thompson would
go for walks and listen for the giggling of small girls.
When he spotted two or three girls playing, he would
follow all of them home and figure out which house
would be the easiest to enter. Typically, he looked for
unlocked or open windows.

After midnight, when the family appeared to be
asleep, Thompson would climb in a window and either
abuse his young victim in her bed or, more frequently,
carry her to a location outside. He told his victims that if
they mentioned the incident to anyone, he would cut off
their legs.

In Illinois Thompson snatched a six-year-old girl who
was sleeping between two younger sisters, carried her to
his truck, and forced her to look at pornographic photographs. He then drove the frightened girl to an isolated
location, performed unspeakable acts, and returned the
victim to her home.

At first, the girl's parents thought her story was just
the product of a young, vivid imagination, but they soon
realized that their daughter was telling the truth. Some
parents in other cities, however, refused to believe the
stories their daughters brought down to the breakfast
table until Thompson was captured and confessed. Although girls in New England and other areas told convincing stories and were visibly traumatized, their
parents assumed the girls had just had horrible nightmares.

We now know that Thompson's victims suffered the worst kind of nightmares: nightmares that happened to be true.

UNLOCKED WINDOWS AND DOORS

Criminals who attack children in their own homes almost always exploit some basic security mistake, such as an unlocked door or window.

In Damascus, Maryland, a stranger entered a home through an unlocked back door, took a two-and-a-half-year old girl out of her crib, abused her in the backyard, and ran off. After the attack, the girl walked back to her house, where her mother found her crying at 6:00 A.M. There was evidence that the man had also been in the parents' bedroom while they slept.

The author has reviewed scores of cases in which child molesters took advantage of unlocked ground-level windows. At an apartment complex in Orange County, Florida, an intruder entered a first-floor window at 4:00 A.M. and raped a nine-year-old girl at knifepoint. The attacker left and the girl screamed for her parents. Investigators told the residents that if they wanted to sleep with open windows, they should buy special locks that keep the windows partly open but prevent criminals from entering.

Child molesters use the same tactics to enter homes and apartments as burglars. In fact, sexual offenders are often burglars who take advantage of an opportunity.

Most families feel safe in keeping second-floor windows open or unlocked; they don't realize that *thousands* of burglars, sex offenders, and other criminals enter homes through second-story windows each year. A twenty-seven-year-old home invader in New Jersey sexually assaulted several young boys in their bedrooms. Utilizing a tactic popular with burglars, the man climbed trees near the homes and entered through unlocked second-floor windows.

Like burglars, many child molesters have also utilized ladders that were stored in the victim's yard or garage. In Wheaton, Maryland, a burglar used a ladder to enter a second-floor window at 5:00 A.M. and attempted a particularly brazen kidnapping of a little girl as her parents slept nearby. After piling a videocassette recorder and other items near the front door, the burglar discovered eight-year-old Karol McCarthy sleeping on the floor next to her parents' bed. The intruder scooped the child off the floor and began to sneak out of the house with the sleeping child in his arms. As he left the bedroom, the man told Karol's twin sister, Megan, to be quiet and not wake up her parents. Fortunately, Karol awoke as the stranger carried her through the kitchen and began screaming. "I thought it was my father but it wasn't," she said in an interview with WRC-TV.

Karol's screams and those of her twin sister awakened their father, Kevin McCarthy, a retired police officer. Shocked out of a deep sleep, he leapt out of the bed, grabbed a handgun, and started chasing the intruder. The burglar managed to carry Karol outside, but dropped her and fled when Mr. McCarthy ordered him to stop.

GUARD YOUR KEYS

Many bedroom attacks on children have occurred after sex offenders have surreptitiously obtained keys to the victims' homes. A woman who had her purse stolen at work learned that the thief used her house keys to enter her home and then raped her thirteen-year-old daughter. In 1993 at least 1,200 purses were stolen from the workplace. An eight-year-old boy was fondled in his basement one week after his family moved into their new home. The offender had once rented a room in the same house and the victim's family had neglected to change the locks when they moved in. It is important to remember that many child molesters have jobs that bring them into contact with the victims. Every year scores of children are victimized by sex offenders who have previously worked as gardeners, carpet cleaners, repairmen, and so forth in their homes. Many of these workmen stole or duplicated the keys they were issued when they performed their duties.

Children Lured Into Vehicles

Four blocks from the Catholic elementary school, a man wearing a tie, sunglasses, and a baseball hat pulled his blue van up to the curb, leaned across the front seat, and opened the passenger-side door. "Excuse me, girls," he said to two sixth-graders. "Can you tell me how I get to the elementary school?" It was Monday morning, May 17, and the girls were both carrying book bags and wearing matching skirts and blouses, uniforms required at their school. The girls could see that the man was holding a map but, at first, could not hear what he was saying. As the sixth-graders moved closer to the vehicle, the man, who would later be described as "about the same age as my daddy," slid across the front seat and stood with one leg in the vehicle and one leg on the curb. "Denise, can you tell me where the elementary school is located?" Disarmed that the stranger knew her

name, Denise remembered thinking that he must have
been a friend of her parents. Maureen, the second girl,
now assumed that Denise knew the man. "Yes, sir," Denise responded in her usual polite way, "the school is
right over that way."

Police now conjecture that the man, who fit the description of a suspect wanted in three other child abductions, probably considered two options. Maybe he would
get lucky, as he had three weeks earlier, and the girls
would offer to get in the car and show him the way.
After all, as Denise would later report, "He didn't look
mean or anything." The man, of course, fully realized
that the girls were going to the same location he was
allegedly trying to find. His second option, the police
guessed, was to grab one or both of the girls and force
them into the van.

"We would never have gotten into a stranger's car,"
Maureen later said in an interview. The friendly man
with the big smile who somehow knew Denise's name
was forced to resort to option number two.

As Denise stood by the vehicle door and pointed directions, first left and then right with her finger, the man
suddenly grabbed her around the waist and pulled her
roughly into the van, cutting Denise's forehead on the
roof while doing so.

Maureen reached in the van and tried to grab her
friend's legs but was shoved forcefully backward. The
man slammed and locked the passenger-side door and
sped away, holding Denise's head to the front seat with
his right hand.

Mature beyond her years and considered the best
reader in her class, Maureen at this point did something
incredible: she wrote down the license plate number of
the vehicle. She then ran to the first house she could

find and pounded on the door. Nobody home. Now crying, Maureen ran next door and frantically rang the doorbell. A woman answered the door and the distraught child said, "Call 911, someone stole my friend." The woman handed the phone to Maureen and the dispatcher relayed her information to the officers on patrol.

Pushed out of the car one hour later, the longest hour in her young life, Denise was disheveled and dazed. She too knocked on a door and asked for help. She too was crying.

A psychiatrist explained that it was normal for Denise to be unable to remember many details about the man or the rape. "She was in shock and mentally anesthetized herself while she was being attacked."

Police traced the blue van to a rental agency. It had been rented in another state with stolen credit cards. When the abandoned vehicle was discovered mired in mud, investigators found Denise's book bag and socks. The name "Denise" was printed in big letters on the book bag, explaining how the stranger knew the girl's name. Another article of Denise's clothing was still missing. The psychiatrist believes that the assailant probably kept this particular piece of clothing as a souvenir. "If you ever catch this creep you'll probably find he has lots of souvenirs," the psychiatrist told the author.

Denise and her parents are naturally concerned because her address was in her book bag and the kidnapper's last words were "Tell anyone and I'll kill you . . . I know where you live."

This man, this "creep," who is *known* to have pulled three young girls and a seven-year-old boy into his car, is still at large.

More than 3,000 girls and boys will be abducted this year—some short-term, some long-term—by criminals who lure or drag them into vehicles.

Start with the basics. Teach your children that they should never accept a ride with a stranger. Never get into a vehicle with a man or woman of any age, for any reason, if you and your family do not know that person.

It is important to teach children the tactics that child molesters and other criminals might use to lure them into a vehicle.

As we have just seen, many kidnappers will pull their vehicles to the curb and ask a child for directions. If someone calls out to the child and asks, "How do I get to the playground?" or "Can you tell me where the school is located?" the child should move in the opposite direction the vehicle is headed so he or she cannot be grabbed. Adults rarely ask children for assistance, they ask other adults. If a child chooses to respond, he or she should do it quickly ("It's straight ahead two blocks") and move *away* from the vehicle. They should never engage the motorist in conversation.

In Alexandria, Virginia, on May 1, 1994, an eleven-year-old girl was riding her bicycle when a male motorist held out a letter and asked if she would please put it in a nearby mailbox. As the girl reached for the letter, the man grabbed her and pulled her into his car. The girl was driven to a wooded area, forced to drink two beers, and then undressed and raped. The suspect arrested for this crime is believed to have molested or raped thirty other children in Maryland, Virginia, and Washington, D.C.

Another child molester who pulled thirteen girls and boys into his car typically obtained the names of neighborhood children and then asked passing boys and girls,

"Excuse me, do you know Jane Smith?" or "Do you know Johnny Jones?" When the child responded in the affirmative, the man asked, "Would you please give these crayons [or a ball] to her?" As the children reached for the crayons or ball, the man pulled them into his vehicle.

It is not advisable to write the child's name in big letters on his or her lunch box, book bag, or jacket; child molesters frequently use the name to feign familiarity. "Denise, can you tell me where the elementary school is located?" Since there are many ways a criminal can obtain a child's name (they could hear another child calling to the targeted child, "Hey, Timmy, wait up!"), tell children not to be tricked if a stranger uses their name. This is important because several victims have admitted that they were embarrassed to admit that they did not recognize someone who knew their names. "I pretended that I knew him because he knew my name," one victim admitted to the police. As in Denise's case, many children assume that the stranger is a friend of their parents if their name is used. One child molester called out a girl's name and told her he was a relative; the girl believed him. It is easy for the "bad guys" to learn a child's name.

Tell children the truth. Most people in the world are good. But most children have seen enough television and have had enough life experiences to figure out that some people are "bad." And bad people are quite willing to tell lies to trick children.

In Santa Ana, California, nine-year-old Nadia Puente was lured into a car near her school by a thirty-five-year-old man who said he was a teacher. Nadia was kidnapped, raped, and murdered. Her body was found stuffed in a garbage can in Griffith Park. The truth is that some people tell lies. An eleven-year-old girl was lured to a shopping mall and killed by a man who said he worked with the girl's mother.

Several child molesters have approached children and feigned an emergency of some sort. "Your mother is in the hospital and I'm supposed to bring you to her," said one convicted pedophile. Pulling up to a school bus stop, another child molester told a seven-year-old boy, "Your father asked me to drive you home." The boy obediently got in the car. Parents should select a code word that only they and their children know. If a stranger does not know the code word, the children will know not to trust him or her.

Inform children that criminals are often very clever and use props to make themselves appear legitimate or official. A criminal who stops a car to ask directions may hold a map in his hands. A criminal who wants to show you the puppies in his van may be holding a leash. Child molesters use many different props. One man who offered rides to boys who were carrying baseball gloves wore a whistle around his neck, a baseball hat, and a T-shirt that said "Coach" on the front.

Explain to children that real life is different from television. In real life the "bad guys" are often well dressed and friendly. The bad guy may not seem mean. "He didn't look mean or anything," said Denise. Criminals can be male or female, black or white, young or old.

In over one hundred recorded cases, kidnappers have asked children for some kind of assistance with their car or van. Standing by his van with the hood up, one man asked a twelve-year-old boy to "turn the key in the ignition" while he fiddled with the engine. As the child molester knew, the offer made the boy feel important and the ruse got the boy inside the van. Another child molester asked a Girl Scout to help him look under his car because "I think I just ran over a cat." As the girl looked under his car, the man grabbed her.

Child molesters have used every type of vehicle, but children should be especially wary of vans. From the criminal's point of view, vans are operationally perfect. Criminals can enter or exit vans from the front, back, and sides. (The back and side doors make it easy to pull someone in, especially if the criminals are working in pairs.) Vans offer a lot of room inside and are often disguised to look like delivery vehicles or utility service vans. Because it is difficult to see inside a van, it is the perfect hiding place for accomplices. Also, once a child is lured into a van, the height of the vehicle and/or the lack of windows makes it nearly impossible to signal for help or to be seen. Children should never accept invitations to see something in a van (like barking puppies) and should not accept money to help a stranger load boxes into a van. Both of these tactics have been used many times.

Perhaps the most frightening tactic being used against children is the impersonation of police. A wide range of criminals pretending to be police victimize 25,000 men, women, and children each year in the United States. The police impersonation tactic is used by con artists, kidnappers, sex offenders, serial murderers, and other types of criminals.

The author has recorded 915 cases in which criminals pretending to be police officers have victimized children, and the trend seems to be increasing. The encouraging news is that scores of children have refused to be fooled by this trick. Awareness of the police impersonation tactic is the most important first step: a child who is informed that criminals sometimes use this trick is less likely to be caught off guard.

Interestingly, many victims of the police impersonation tactic later admit that they knew something was "fishy" or wrong with the situation. Children should be taught to listen to their instincts; if something feels wrong it probably is wrong. Children should also be taught that it is okay to say no to some adults.

In Gaithersburg, Maryland, a man put a red light on the dashboard of his car and pulled his vehicle alongside two twelve-year-old girls walking down the street. The man ordered one of the girls into his car where she was handcuffed, driven to a secluded area, and sexually abused.

In nonemergency situations, it is rare that a legitimate officer in plainclothes will ask a child to get into an unmarked vehicle. We want to avoid the situations in which a child automatically jumps into an unmarked car simply because a stranger flashes a badge and claims to be a police officer. A child should refuse to get in an unmarked vehicle with a plainclothes "police officer" until he or she has checked with a parent, teacher, or another adult. In the vast majority of cases, if a child seems wise to a possible trick, an impostor will drive off.

Regardless of how the would-be abductor operates, children should be taught to resist. If someone grabs or attempts to grab them, they should scream, kick, bite, and call for help as loudly as possible. Most child molesters look for an easy, submissive target; they do not want to attract attention. There are scores of recorded cases in which children have escaped or been rescued when their fighting and screaming attracted attention.

Bus Stops

Jaycee Lee Dugard was eleven years old in 1991 when a man and a woman dragged her into a car while she waited at her school bus stop, one block from her home in Lake Tahoe, California. Standing in his driveway, Jaycee's father witnessed the abduction. He saw his shy, blue-eyed daughter being pulled into the car, frantically ran up the street to rescue her, and was forced to watch helplessly as the car disappeared. The pretty, blond-haired girl with a "butterfly" birthmark on her right arm and a noticeable gap between her front teeth is still missing. In a meeting with the author in 1994, Jaycee's mother bravely explained that she would never give up the search for her daughter, but sadly admitted that there had been no encouraging leads.

Since Jaycee was abducted, more than 600 other children nationwide have been stalked and approached at bus stops. On January 14, 1992, a fourteen-year-old girl was abducted from a bus stop in Brooklyn, New York, and raped by two men. At 7:00 A.M. the slender, dark-haired teenager was alone at the bus stop when a man walked up to her and grabbed her around the neck. Telling her he had a gun, the man forced the girl into a car that was driven by a second man. During her ordeal the men told the girl that they had been watching her for several mornings. After being released, the girl provided police with the license plate number, which was traced to a stolen car.

During February 1994 there were a series of abductions and attempted abductions of children in the Boston area. In several cases, the man pulled over at bus stops, opened the driver's side door, and called out to the children, ages five to fourteen. Using typical lures, the man asked if the children wanted to see his puppy, if they wanted a ride, or if they would help search for a lost dog.

Recognizing that children are often targeted at bus stops, it would help immensely if we all kept an eye on these locations. Many communities ask retired adults and other volunteers to watch bus stops in the morning and afternoon. These people watch for loitering strangers and for motorists who appear to be stalking the children. If they reside near a school bus stop, many parents and volunteers will stand in their yards as a visible deterrent. Child molesters try to avoid witnesses.

Children who have to wait at isolated bus stops alone or in small groups, day after day, are particularly vulnerable, especially if they wait in the dark. If a bus stop is surrounded by woods or other hiding places, pedophiles are certain to find it. An additional danger exists when children must walk through woods, a park, or a sparsely populated area to get to and from the bus stop.

Children should be told about the potential dangers associated with bus stops. If a person they do not know continues to ask them even innocent questions, they should tell a teacher or parent. They should never get into a stranger's car. Child molesters will frequently show up at bus stops when it is raining or snowing and offer rides. They have also been known to claim that the bus has broken down and that they have been sent around to pick up the children. Instruct children to watch for people who might be following them when they walk home from the bus stop; even if they do not appear to be menacing, reporting such occurrences can avert greater tragedies.

Sometimes parents have had to get a little more involved, a little more aggressive. In Grand Rapids, Michigan, a woman who police called "super mom" staked out her ten-year-old daughter's bus stop with a camera after the girl complained she was harassed three times by a stranger. After receiving the complaint, police watched the bus stop for a couple days but called off the surveillance when the suspect failed to appear. That's when "super mom" went into action. Armed with binoculars and a camera with a zoom lens, the woman waited patiently until the man approached her daughter for a fourth time. As her daughter ran for the house the woman snapped photos; when the man drove off, the woman chased him in her own car, reaching speeds of seventy-five miles per hour. "Super mom" recorded the man's license plate and police arrested a convicted rapist who had just been released from prison. The man, who had served only nine years of a twenty-one-year sentence, has now been charged with assault with intent to commit kidnapping.

Shopping Malls

John Walsh is the host of *America's Most Wanted*, an award-winning television program that has helped authorities capture scores of wanted fugitives. John Walsh is also a father who lost a six-year-old son.

Like most summer days in Hollywood, Florida, the Monday morning of July 27, 1981, was sunny and comfortable. John, then an executive with a hotel management firm, gave a good-bye kiss to his beautiful wife Reve, hugged his son Adam, and headed out for the office. Reve and Adam went shopping at a nearby mall.

Browsing in a department store, Reve allowed Adam to play in the toy section while she searched for a living-room lamp. When she returned a few minutes later to check on Adam, he was gone. Walking briskly from aisle to aisle, Reve searched the store for her little "Kooter," who was wearing a red baseball cap. Now running full speed, Reve desperately searched the parking lot and surrounding stores. She had Adam paged on the public-address system. Where could he be?

In a panic, Reve called John at his office.

"Adam's lost," she frantically reported. John was at the mall within fifteen minutes.

As morning turned to night, John and Reve sat in a police station and tried to come to grips with the horrible realization that their only child had probably been abducted.

The next morning, with a massive search still ongoing, the Walshes began doing television interviews pleading for their son's return. "Adam," his mother said, "don't be afraid. We love you."

Hearing about the Walshes' plight, ABC's *Good Morning America* invited the parents to New York to be on the program. The night before the show, John and Reve met with the producer and Julie Patz, another panelist, whose son, Etan, had been missing for nearly six years.

After pleading for help on the *Good Morning America* show, the Walshes returned to their hotel room. The telephone rang. It was the Hollywood police.

Part of a child's corpse had been discovered in a swamp more than one hundred miles from Hollywood, Florida. Using dental records, the remains were positively identified as those of Adam Walsh, age six. The search had come to a tragic end and every parent's worst nightmare had come true for Reve and John Walsh.

Turning paralyzing grief into action, the Walshes have dedicated their lives to efforts that will help make children safe from strangers.

Pedophiles and other people who prey on children are naturally drawn to shopping malls. In fact, it is safe to assume that at any given shopping mall, on any given day, there is at least one person who would sexually abuse or kidnap your child if given the opportunity. Thousands of offenses against children, including rape, kidnapping, and murder, are reported at shopping malls and department stores each year in the United States.

The problem has existed for a long time. In 1975 the two young daughters of a well-known radio announcer disappeared from the Wheaton Plaza shopping center in Maryland. They have never been found.

Katherine and Sheila Lyon, ages eleven and thirteen, were given two dollars each and permission to browse around the shopping center. It was noontime on a Tuesday and schools were closed for spring break. The beautiful and vivacious young girls were last seen talking with a well-dressed man in his fifties who was holding a microphone attached to a tape recorder. Although the man was never caught, he had reportedly approached many young girls at suburban shopping centers, using his tape recorder and a false story to initiate a conversation.

Children are criminally victimized in shopping malls every day in the United States. In 1993 a five-year-old girl was abducted from a shopping mall in Schaumburg, Illinois, when she wandered away from her father. The fifty-four-year-old male kidnapper had dressed like a woman and had also kidnapped a six-year-old girl a week earlier in Ohio. As is so often the case, the kidnapper had a history of pedophilia and had recently been paroled after serving a prison term for kidnapping three other children.

Crimes against children in shopping malls are not always committed by adults; amazingly, sometimes the perpetrators are children. Who could ever forget the scene, recorded by security cameras and shown by every major television network in Europe and the United States, of two ten-year-old boys escorting a toddler out of a shopping mall in Liverpool, England. While the mother of the toddler paid for a purchase, the boys led the two-year-old boy outside, stoned him to death, and left him on a railroad track to be run over by a train.

Leaving a young child unattended in a shopping mall can be extremely risky. If a stranger politely offers to watch your child for you, do not accept; even innocent-looking grandmothers have stolen children. Never leave your child unattended in the car while you are shopping; many children have been abducted when left in cars "just for a minute." Children have been abducted when parents and baby-sitters were purchasing items or trying on clothes. All children and teenagers should be advised never to leave the mall with a stranger. In dozens of recorded cases, serial murderers (many prey on children) and child molesters have pretended to be photographers representing modeling agencies or teen magazines. They often ask their victims to go outside to "sign a release form" or "to find a more picturesque setting." Children and teens should be taught to be skeptical of such people and refuse to leave the mall with them. Teenagers with driver's licenses should be told to be very leery of police impersonators who approach them in malls and say, "There's been an accident with your car . . . would you come out to the parking lot please." Think! There are hundreds of people in the mall. How would an "officer" know to whom the car belongs? Only a stalker would know. It is also likely that the criminal does not know what type of car his/her victim is driving; the criminal might be relying on panic to lure the victim out to the parking lot. Teenagers and adults alike should be advised that criminals frequently flatten tires in mall parking lots and then magically appear and offer a ride. No one should accept a ride from a stranger. Remember too, criminals are not always men. Children and teenagers have frequently let down their guards and been lured from shopping malls by women. As incredible as it may seem, many pedophiles and serial murderers have had female accomplices.

Quoted in the *Washington Times,* the wife of the salesman who sexually abused ten girls on a showroom floor stated: "I just wanted to send a message to parents not to trust anybody. He's a well educated, attractive man. If you're a pedophile, it doesn't mean that you look ugly."

Playgrounds, Parks, and Fairs

The camera pans across a playground that looks like a thousand other playgrounds. The viewer sees children playing on swings and seesaws. A little girl with braided hair screams with glee as she glides down a shiny sliding board into a pile of sawdust. As a zoom lens provides a close-up look of a barefooted, eight-year-old boy, a narrator begins his monologue: "Some people go to shopping malls to find what they need. . . . This is where I shop, this is where I hunt, this is where I find my boys."

This scary scene was from a pornographic videotape that was confiscated by law enforcement authorities from the apartment of a known child molester. The two "producers" of this horrible video had conspired to kidnap a young boy from a playground and then film him being sexually abused as part of a pornographic snuff film. The script called for the boy to be murdered on camera. Fortunately, the would-be kidnappers were convicted of the plot and are now serving long prison terms.

Each year, thousands of innocent children are molested or abducted from playgrounds, parks, and fairs in the United States. Most of the predators at these playgrounds and parks are known sexual offenders who were previously given suspended sentences or released early from prison terms.

In Plano, Texas, seven-year-old Ashley Nicole Estell was murdered after being abducted from a public park where hundreds of people were attending a soccer tournament. Michael Blair, the twenty-three-year-old carpet cleaner charged with the abduction, should have still been in prison at the time of Ashley's kidnapping. He had been serving a ten-year prison sentence for breaking into an apartment and assaulting an eleven-year-old girl but had been released early by mistake. The young victim awoke to find Blair kissing and fondling her. He fled when the girl screamed but, incredibly, returned a week later and tried to pull the same girl through a window. If Blair had served his full ten-year sentence for that attack, instead of being released after only eighteen months, Ashley Nicole Estell would still be enjoying parks and playgrounds with her friends.

Our playgrounds and parks would also have been a lot safer for our children if Westley Allen Dodd had not been allowed to roam free. Over and over again for seventeen years Dodd confessed to molesting children.

And over and over again authorities would reduce the charges, suspend sentence, offer therapy, and release Dodd once again to the playgrounds. He never served more than four months in jail.

Surprisingly candid, Dodd once stated to the media: "Each time I entered treatment, I continued to molest children. I liked molesting children, and did what I had to do to avoid jail so I could continue molesting."

After a one-year child molestation sentence was suspended, Dodd moved to Vancouver, Washington. In Vancouver Dodd returned to his specialty: stalking children at playgrounds, parks, and fairs.

On Labor Day, 1989, shortly after Dodd arrived in Vancouver, he stalked two brothers, William Neer, age ten, and Cole Neer, age eleven, in a neighborhood park. Dodd lured William and Cole to an isolated area, tied them up, molested one child, and then stabbed both boys to death. Seven weeks later Dodd found four-year-old Lee Iseli playing alone in a school yard and lured him to his apartment. Dodd photographed himself repeatedly raping the boy and then strangled and hanged the child.

Captured by police while trying to carry a screaming six-year-old boy from a movie theater, Dodd said that if he ever escaped, "I will kill and rape again and enjoy every minute of it."

After seventeen years authorities finally stopped trying to reform him. On January 5, 1993, the state of Washington executed Westley Allen Dodd by hanging.

Criminals who target children at playgrounds and parks often initiate some sort of game to win the child's confidence and lure the victim into an isolated area. One kidnapper would kick a ball across the playground and entice his potential victim to chase the ball and kick it back. The man would kick the ball a little farther each time until eventually the child had to chase the ball into the woods. A child molester in New York visited parks and challenged children to foot races. The distance of each race got a little longer until eventually the child was out of sight of his or her baby-sitter. In 1993 this child molester, who had recently been released from prison after serving less than half of his sentence, raped and killed a seven-year-old girl.

Another child molester, who operated in five different states, would organize games of hide-and-seek. Carrying a clipboard and wearing a whistle around his neck, this twenty-seven-year-old man appeared legitimate or "official" to many parents and children. When the game began he would separate one child from the rest or convince a boy or girl to "hide over there." Since there are hundreds of parks, school yards, and playgrounds in this molester's five-state area of operation, his "hide-and-seek" tactic could be used over and over. Although he is not known to have killed any children, the man often traumatized his victims for hours.

To initiate touching, pedophiles will sometimes tickle or wrestle with a child or start a game of tag. At a playground in Virginia, an accused child molester convinced a ten-year-old boy to walk into a wooded area, where he asked the boy if he had any cuts or bruises he could look at because he was practicing medicine.

People who molest and abduct children are drawn to fairs, amusement parks, and playgrounds where children gather and are often drawn to jobs that will bring them into contact with children. Since a small percentage of people working in any occupation are likely to have pedophilic tendencies, it should come as no surprise that some vendors and some carnival and amusement park employees are arrested each year for inappropriate behavior with children.

On July 16, 1993, at the Orange Country Fair in Costa Mesa, California, three girls, ages twelve to fourteen, ran from Cactus Jack's Haunted Shack screaming that someone had rubbed his hands over their bodies. Police arrested a forty-one-year-old carnival worker and convicted child molester. When younger children appeared afraid to go through the Haunted Shack, the same worker would offer to take them through. He was charged with a total of nine counts of felony child molestation.

In separate incidents, an ice cream vendor working a park in Leisure City, Florida, was arrested for sexually assaulting four young girls, and a bumper-boat operator at an amusement park in Escondido, California, molested three girls who were at the park on a school field trip.

Many traveling carnivals and circuses make little effort to screen their employees. In several cases, employees arrested for sexual offenses and child abductions in one city have continued to commit the same crimes in town after town.

REDUCING THE RISK

- Lock your doors and windows. The mere presence of a parent in the home will not guarantee a child's safety. Criminals enter an average of 3.2 million homes and apartments each year in the United States. Approximately 800,000 of these home invasions are the result of an unlocked door or window. Each year criminals enter more than 500,000 homes and apartments while at least one family member is present.

- Don't forget about second-story windows. Lock second-floor windows and limit access by trimming back trees, hiding ladders, and eliminating designs and footholds that make your outside wall easy to climb. If you wish to sleep with your windows open, install special locks that keep the windows open but prevent criminals from getting through them.

- Protect your keys. A criminal who has obtained your keys has easy access to you and your children, night and day. If keys are lost or stolen, change your locks. Always change locks when moving into a new residence. If keys are stolen from one parent at work, he/she should immediately notify the parent or baby-sitter who is home with the children. When you have keys duplicated, do not pay with a check that displays your address; a dishonest employee will make one copy for you and one copy for himself. Do not put your name and address on your keys. A word to the wise: *thousands* of keys distributed to workmen, realtors, baby-sitters, housekeepers, etc. have come back to haunt home owners. If you live in an apartment building, tell your manager that you and your *lawyer* are very concerned about passkey security.

- Instruct your children never to answer the door when home alone or to tell anyone over the phone that he/she is alone.

- Never leave a child unattended in a car. A child left in a car is an open invitation to a kidnapper. And remember, if a carjacker steals your car, anything in that car, including children, goes with him. During the last three years forty-three children have been abducted when carjackers stole vehicles.

■ Empower your child with the knowledge that it is okay to say no to some adults. Explain to your children that a stranger is *anyone* they do not know and that they should never get in a car or walk anywhere with a stranger, unless you have given permission.

■ Tell your children never to go with a stranger who offers them money, candy, ice cream, or other bribes. Nor should children eat candy or other foods distributed by strangers at parks, arcades, and movies; some kidnappers use knockout drugs that put the child to sleep.

■ Explain to your children that criminals can look and act like anyone. Tell them that in real life a bad person might be young or old, male or female. The criminal might be very friendly and complimentary and may wear very nice clothes. Many children believe that a stranger is only someone who appears slovenly and speaks harshly.

■ Teach your child to resist. If someone grabs them they should scream, yell for help, bite, kick, and run. They should raise a commotion and attract as much attention as possible. Role-play with your child so he/she can practice resisting and screaming for help. Most kidnappers want an easy submissive victim; they don't want to attract attention.

■ Do not display your child's name on jewelry or on lunch boxes, jackets, etc. A kidnapper seeing the name will be able to approach the child (today or in the future) and create a sense of familiarity. "Hi, Patty, your mother asked me to bring you home." Explain to children that there are many ways a criminal could learn his or her name. You do not go with a stranger or help a stranger just because he or she knows your name.

■ *Hundreds* of children have been abducted by criminals who used puppies, kittens, bunnies, and other animals as props. Parents should be aware of these tactics so they can communicate proper behavior to children. Asking a child to help look for a lost pet is one of the most common tactics used by pedophiles and kidnappers. Often the criminal will carry a leash and a photo of the lost animal. Sometimes the criminal asks a group of children to help and then isolates one child for abduction. A child should never help a stranger look for a lost animal unless a parent has given permission. Several abductions have occurred after a child was invited to see bunnies or kittens in a car or van. A child should never go with a stranger to see animals and should never climb into a strange vehicle. Many children are sexually abused every year after being invited into a house or apartment to play with pets. One child molester allowed children to walk his dog; the dog pulled the children toward the woods.

■ Children should check with their parents before agreeing to do chores or jobs for money. Kidnappers frequently offer children money to help load a car or van. "I'll pay you to help me collect firewood," said a man who lured a boy into the woods. Many offenders have advertised jobs on bulletin boards and in newspapers and then set up "interviews" in isolated areas. Always go on an interview with your child. Be especially cautious if your child has been offered a modeling or acting job. Urge children to inform you if someone has been taking their photograph.

■ Criminals are increasingly pretending to be law enforcement and security personnel. A wide range of criminals victimize more than 25,000 men, women, and children each year in the United States. We want children to be aware of this tactic but not to become paranoid. We want children to depend on the police but not to jump into a stranger's car or be lured from a shopping mall simply because a stranger in plainclothes flashes a badge. If children are aware of this tactic, their instincts will usually tell them when the situation seems wrong. Most impostors leave when confronted by a child who seems assertive and street smart. In a nonemergency situation it would be very unusual for a legitimate officer in plainclothes to ask a child or teenager to get into an unmarked vehicle. A child should refuse to get in an unmarked vehicle with a plainclothes "police officer" or to follow such a person, until a parent, teacher, or another adult has checked out the situation. Children should not leave a shopping mall or a park with someone claiming to be a police officer until a trusted adult or second uniformed officer is called to the scene. Children have been victimized by police impersonators while walking and riding bikes and in every conceivable location including bus stops, malls, and parks.

■ More than 3,000 children will be abducted this year after being lured or dragged into vehicles. Teach your children that they should never get into a vehicle with a man or woman for any reason if you and your family do not know that person. Teach children the tricks that bad people might use to get them near or into a vehicle. "Will you put this letter in the mailbox please?" "Will you please give these crayons to Johnny Jones?" If a motorist asks for directions, asks for the time (if the child is wearing a watch), or says, "Come here please," the child should back away so he/she cannot be grabbed and should move in the opposite direction the vehicle is facing. Never climb into a vehicle to see puppies or for any other reason. Do not help a stranger put things into his car. Do not help an adult fix his car or look for something underneath his car. Explain that some criminals may pretend that there has been an emergency: "Your mother is in the hospital and I am supposed to bring you to her" or "Your father asked me to pick you up." Select a code word that only you and your children know. If a stranger does not know the code word, do not go with him or her. A child can also be told to call home before accepting a ride with anyone. Explain why children should be especially careful around vans.

■ Bus stops are frequently targeted by child molesters and other criminals. Children should be taught to be aware of motorists and pedestrians who approach them at a bus stop and should tell an adult if someone harasses them or follows them to or from a bus stop. Explain to children that criminals frequently offer rides on rainy days and sometimes claim that "the bus broke down, I'll give you a lift." We can all help by keeping an eye on children at bus stops and by reporting suspicious activities to the police.

■ People who prey on children naturally gravitate to playgrounds, parks, and fairs. Children should be instructed to play with children about their own age and never to leave a park or playground with a stranger for any reason. Since criminals use so many different tactics, it is important when instructing your children to role-play and to be very specific. Present real-life situations that have actually occurred at playgrounds and parks and instruct your child on the proper response. If a man asks you to help him find a puppy, what will you do? What would you do if someone offered you money to go with him? If a stranger wants to take you somewhere to buy you an ice cream cone, what would you say? Suppose a stranger wants to race you across the field, what would you do? If a man in a car calls you over to him, how would you handle that? Point out areas of the playground where children should not play.

■ Shopping malls pose special risks. Never leave a child unattended in a shopping mall, even for a minute. If someone politely offers to watch your child, politely refuse. Be aware if someone distracts your attention; kidnappers sometimes work in pairs. Explain to older children and teenagers that criminals use many tricks to lure them outside or into isolated sections of the mall. Children should be very cautious if they are approached by photographers, modeling agents, writers for teen magazines, or people in plainclothes claiming to be police or security officers. In any confusing or uncomfortable situation, encourage your child to ask a salesclerk or an adult shopper for help. Children who would not leave a shopping center with an adult male often throw caution to the wind when approached by a woman or a young teenager. Tell children that a stranger is *anyone* they do not know including other children.

■ Teach your children *how* and *when* to call 911. Steven Stayner was abducted by a pedophile when he was seven years old and held until he escaped at age fourteen. Stayner relates that he could have summoned help many times when he was first kidnapped but at age seven he did not know how the telephone worked. In hundreds of recorded cases children, ages two to thirteen, have saved themselves and others by calling 911. First, teach your child his or her full name and address. Children should also know your first and last name, especially if your last names are different. Unplug your real phone and have your child call 911. Role-playing, the parent should play the part of a dispatcher and ask what is the problem, what is your name, what is your address. (Even if your child can't relay his/her address, many 911 services can trace your number and address.) Tell your child reasons he/she should call 911. ("I'm lost." "There's a fire." "Someone is hurt.") Also teach your children reasons they should not call 911, i.e., you do not call to find out if the snowstorm canceled classes. Tape your address and phone number next to the phone.

- Prepare an emergency kit. Keep several copies of current, high-quality photographs that clearly show front and side views of your child's face. New photos should be taken at least once a year. Produce an up-to-date videotape that features your child's voice and mannerisms. Various video outlets offer this service if you do not have your own equipment. Have your children fingerprinted. In most communities the local police will either do this for you or tell you where it can be done. Always make a mental note of what your child is wearing.

Child Molesters:
Facts About
Pedophiles

A pedophile is a person who is sexually attracted to children.* Pedophiles are usually male but can also be female and can be of any sexual persuasion, i.e., heterosexual, homosexual, or bisexual. Although estimates vary, there are probably at least 4 million practicing pedophiles in the United States.

Sexual exploitation of children by pedophiles can take many forms, i.e., molestation and rape, incest (more than 300,000 female and male children are sexually abused by a family member each year), pornography, and child prostitution. Child pornography is a $500-million-per-year business.

Pedophiles are found in all professions. They have been known to be pediatricians, priests, pilots, plumbers, police officers, and photographers. Pedophiles have

---

* Technically, a pedophile is attracted to prepubescent boys and girls. People who are sexually attracted to youngsters in puberty or just emerging are called ephebophiles.

been Boy Scout leaders, teachers, coaches, day-care providers, athletes, and entertainers.

Photographs and writings found among the effects of Lord Robert Baden-Powell, war hero and founder of the Boy Scouts of America; Sir James Barrie, author of *Peter Pan;* and Lewis Carroll, author of *Alice In Wonderland,* strongly suggest that these men were pedophiles, though there is no proof they acted on their obsessions.

Many experts estimate that at least three percent of the males in any profession have pedophilic tendencies. Less than one percent of the females have pedophilic tendencies. Almost half of the known child molesters in the United States have used their professions to gain access to child victims. Stated another way, about fifty percent of the known child molesters have gravitated to professions and jobs that will give them easy access to children.

Pedophiles can be from any race or socio-economic background. A high percentage of pedophiles are white, middle- to upper-class males, who work in skilled and white-collar professions. Pedophiles can range in age from their late teens to their late seventies.

Most pedophiles believe that their sexuality is natural, harmless, and an integral part of their personality and would not change even if there were a cure. They believe that pedophilia is a sexual preference like heterosexuality or homosexuality and that it is not an illness.

Although most pedophiles prefer to operate in privacy behind closed doors, children are increasingly being groped and molested in crowded swimming pools, movie theaters, elevators, and other public areas. In several recorded cases children have been blatantly abused by store employees while parents shopped nearby. During March 1994 police in Fairfax, Virginia, arrested a thirty-one-year-old man and charged him with fondling ten young girls, ages two to seven, while he was on duty as a salesman at Luskin's department store. Using store video equipment, the man filmed himself sexually abusing the children on the showroom of the electronics store. The man's wife gave the tape to police after finding it in her home, hidden beneath a bureau. Shocked by what she saw on the tape—her husband pulling down a little girl's pants in the middle of a store without anyone noticing—the twenty-nine-year-old wife felt obligated to protect future victims. Each of the molestations occurred as parents of the victims shopped nearby for a television, microwave oven, or other electronics equipment. A mother of two young girls, quoted in *The Washington Post,* said she remembers one salesman offering her girls a chair to watch a movie. "Don't worry. We'll keep an eye on them," the salesman said.

Already furious, the parents of the ten victims got even angrier when they learned that the salesman had been convicted of a similar offense six years earlier at the Sears Automotive Center at Montgomery Mall in Maryland. In that case, the salesman fondled a six-year-old girl who was sitting alone in a lounge area watching a movie as her parents browsed nearby. Another employee walked by and could not believe what he was seeing. The salesman had his hand under the girl's dress. When the employee yelled at the salesman to stop, he got no response. The salesman appeared hypnotized by what he was doing and did not seem to fear getting caught. The employee yelled again, and the salesman stopped.

Most experts believe that there is no "cure" for pedophilia; it can be arrested but never fully eradicated. Therefore, known child molesters should not have unsupervised access to children even if they have received therapy.

Contrary to popular belief, most male adults who sexually abuse young boys are not homosexual in their adult relationships. In fact, male pedophiles who are attracted to boy victims typically report that they are repulsed or uninterested in adult homosexual relationships. At least eighty percent of the male adults who exploit children sexually are heterosexual (mostly) or bisexual in their adult relationships.

For years, the Boy Scouts of America tried to protect Scouts from sex abuse by screening out men who were gay. But today the Scouts distribute the "Youth Protection Guidelines" that says it is a "myth" that "children are at greater risk of sexual victimization from gay adults than straight adults." Ironically, while the Boy Scouts of America were guarding for gays, at least 1,800 heterosexual pedophiles infiltrated their ranks.

A high percentage of pedophiles are married and have children of their own. These men usually have sexual relationships with adult women, but children (either boys, girls, or both) are their primary sexual interest.

Although it is true that thousands of children have been abducted and forcibly assaulted by strangers, almost eighty percent of all sexual offenses against children are committed by a family member or someone who is known and has a close relationship with the child.

Most sexual offenses against children, including intercourse and oral sex, do not involve physical force. Most sexual offenses against children involve a seduction process: enticements, persuasion, affection, rewards, cajolement, flattery, gifts, and much needed attention. But a pedophile may also use threats, guilt, bribes, pressure, blackmail, entrapment, or adult authority to lure children into a sexual relationship.

Pedophiles are masters at the seduction process and offenders are usually considered great with kids. "Kids love me," said David Lee Thompson who molested children in a dozen states. Pedophiles have the ability to communicate at the youngster's level and show a great deal of empathy and knowledge concerning the child's interests. They are very good at listening and paying attention to children, an ability many parents lack. Pedophiles know the "in" games, television shows, toys, and movies. In short, pedophiles are skilled at recognizing a child's emotional needs and are willing to invest all the time necessary to seduce the child.

It is important to understand the ploys and tactics that pedophiles use. Bit by bit, pedophiles try to manipulate situations so that they are alone with the child. A determined child molester will always find a way to isolate and seduce a child. Frequently they will tell parents that they are taking several children on a trip or to a ball game; at the last minute everyone but the targeted child mysteriously "cancels." Some pedophiles have even dated single mothers so that they will eventually be trusted to be alone with the child.

A pedophile will try to get a child in a position where they are changing clothes together, showering together, or staying overnight together. They will try to exploit a child's natural curiosity about sex and will frequently show the child pornographic films or magazines. Many pedophiles ply their victim with drugs and alcohol and some have utilized knockout drugs that put the child to sleep or render him helpless. Some arrange situations so that they are napping together and some molest children when they are asleep. Showering a child with gifts is also a common seduction ploy.

Massages, strip poker (and other strip games), tickling, "touchy-feelie" games, and games that require a blindfold play a large role in the seduction process.

Pornography and photography also play a big role in the seduction process. Hundreds of parents each year are stunned to learn that trusted friends, family members, baby-sitters, teachers, and others have taken pornographic photos of their children. These photos may be distributed or used for the pedophile's personal stimulation. Frequently they are sold or exchanged with other pedophiles. Sometimes the pedophile tricks the child into posing, sometimes he or she pays the child, and sometimes the photos are taken surreptitiously.

One pedophile sponsored skinny-dipping parties at his pool (he would suggest going swimming when he knew the children did not have swimming suits), and another pedophile instructed boys in complicated wrestling moves. First-aid lessons and physicals are commonly used as excuses to touch a child's buttocks and genitals.

Because of the taboo nature of pedophilia, secrecy plays a large role in the seduction process. They may say "this is our little secret" or they may threaten harm if the child tells.

Sadly, thousands of children each year learn about sex from a pedophile. A trusted and well-liked adult tells them "it's okay" and the child believes him. The pedophile commits the unkindest cut of all: breach of trust.

On the average, by the time a pedophile has been arrested he has already molested fifty children. The most vulnerable children are the ones who lack parental affection and love. Pedophiles are adept at finding these children. They are adept at finding children who feel badly. If a child is starving for adult affection, he or she is very likely to succumb to a pedophile's seduction.

There is no such thing as a profile of a pedophile. There are many behaviors that are common among child molesters, but these same behaviors are exhibited by people who are not pedophiles.

Pedophiles tend to move from place to place (they are often run out of town), and their best friends tend to be children. Pedophiles are excessively active in Boy Scouts, Big Brothers, Little League, and other youth groups and continually put themselves in a position to befriend children. One pedophile was coaching four youth teams at once and was molesting children on all four teams. Many pedophiles are vague about their backgrounds but they have a knack for getting people to trust them.

The only way to predict if a man or woman will molest a child in the future is to find out if that person has sexually abused a child in the past.

The one characteristic that is common to all pedophiles is that they do great harm to children. Sexually abused children almost always suffer serious emotional and psychological problems that carry over into adulthood.

When a pedophile touches a child's body, he is also touching a mind and a soul. A pedophile kills a child's spirit.

Someone You Know

In a courtroom in Santa Ana, California, Edward Cho, a successful fifty-four-year-old businessman, hung his head and listened as his twenty-year-old daughter finally had her say. Quoted in the *Los Angeles Times,* the young woman said, "I want you to know, Dad, that I am a person and not an object." Although obviously full of rage and on the verge of tears, the woman stood tall and spoke in a loud, clear voice. "It's really hard for me to call you 'Dad.' I really want to deny it. . . . It makes me really sick to know you're my dad."

Mr. Cho was convicted of twenty-five counts of rape, molestation, and assault against his own three daughters, including his twenty-three-year-old daughter who committed suicide a year earlier. The sexual abuse began when the girls were ten to fourteen years old.

Mr. Cho was sentenced December 10, 1993, to eighty-four years in prison. The two surviving daughters and a son then launched a civil lawsuit against Cho and his wife, alleging that she did nothing to protect them as children. Mr. Cho will be eligible for parole when he is ninety-five years old.

Eighty percent of all sexual crimes against children are committed by a relative or someone they know; a parent or grandparent; a stepfather or a mother's boyfriend; an uncle or a brother-in-law; a baby-sitter, a baby-sitter's boyfriend, or the next-door neighbor. Most people are not child molesters. In fact, most healthy adults would risk their lives to protect your child from such harm. But there is no denying the truth. The people a child spends the most time with are the people most likely to sexually abuse that child.

Millions of incidents over the years have proven to researchers that "someone you know" is a greater sexual threat to your children than the stereotypical stranger who wears a trench coat and foams at the mouth. This is not something most parents want to believe; it's an uncomfortable truth.

We have been led to believe that if a person has a kind demeanor, then he or she must be psychologically healthy. We have been led to believe that if a person occupies a position of authority, or is friendly toward us, then that person can be trusted with our children. The data tells us that this is not always the case.

In 1993 the author recorded nearly 10,000 cases in which children were sexually abused by someone they knew.

The abusers in this sampling of 10,000 incidents included friends, fathers, stepfathers, grandfathers, baby-sitters, boyfriends, uncles, godfathers, brothers-in-law, and neighbors.

Although child abuse data is being processed in computers, many experts worry that the findings are not always being processed by parents. Parents are taking precautions to protect children from strangers but are often ignoring a greater "Someone You Know" danger. The following five incidents, reported in 1993, are taken from our sampling of 10,000 cases and are intended to communicate today's reality of child abuse:

Lancaster, California. A twelve-year-old girl announced that she was suing her twenty-nine-year-old godfather who was convicted of sexually assaulting her. The girl said she is suing so that other children will come forward and so that parents will realize "it does happen."

Ebensburg, Pennsylvania. A sixteen-year-old girl and her eighteen-year-old boyfriend were found guilty of charges that they engaged in sexual acts with young children they were baby-sitting. The two were arrested after a father found his six-year-old daughter and four-year-old son engaged in oral sex. The children said they learned the acts from the baby-sitter and her boyfriend. The teenagers also took pornographic photos of the children.

Houston, Texas. A grandfather was charged with sexually assaulting his eight-year-old granddaughter. The victim told her mother that when everyone else went outside to watch fireworks on July 4, her grandfather touched his genitals to hers. The little girl told her mother that her grandfather had been molesting her for some time.

Canton, Georgia. A sixteen-year-old teenager was charged with raping his four-year-old niece, whom he was baby-sitting. The teenager's mother came home and found the little girl in tears.

Taneytown, Maryland. A fifty-four-year-old man was sentenced to thirteen years in prison for sexually abusing his teenaged stepdaughter. The abuse, which included intercourse, started when the child was three years old and continued until she was fifteen. Typically, the man would wait until his wife was out of the house and then would take his stepdaughter into his bedroom.

In 1971 Karen Hartman was only five years old but she remembers her stepfather having sex with her older sisters. By the time she was eight years old, Karen too was having sexual intercourse with her father. Quoted in *The Miami Herald,* in an article by Mary Hargrove, Karen said, "I saw my sisters doing it and I just figured . . . he was my father and that's how it was."

Cindy, Karen's sister, remembers having sex with her father at least once a week from the time she was in third grade until she left home at eighteen years old. "We were afraid of him," she explained.

Today the girls still remember the abuse, they still suffer certain psychological problems, but they are not afraid.

In 1993 the girls had their fifty-five-year-old father arrested. "This happened a long time ago," he reportedly stated to the Florida detective who arrested him. "I thought it was all forgotten and forgiven."

A victim of child abuse can never forget. "You need to face it," said Cindy. "Until you take care of it, it will stay with you forever."

Pedophilia in the Religious Community

Pedophilia is a problem in almost all religions: Catholic, Jewish, Baptist, Buddhist, Episcopal, Lutheran, Presbyterian, Methodist, Mennonite, Mormon, Muslim, and so forth. The percentage of clergymen or religious leaders who are practicing pedophiles is roughly the same percentage that exists in the rest of society. *Most clergymen and religious leaders do not molest children.* Since there are scores of religions represented in the United States this "three to four percent" means that there are many thousands of religious leaders who should not have unsupervised access to children.

In 1988 three Georgia evangelists pleaded guilty to charges that they used traveling revivals and the Lighthouse Assembly to lure hundreds of boys across the Southeast into homosexual prostitution. Many parents of the victims allowed their sons to follow the evangelists because they thought they were being trained for the ministry. Mario "Tonny" Leyva, one of the convicted ministers, admitted he sexually molested more than one hundred boys, some as young as eight years old, during his twenty years as a revivalist.

Every week a new scandal involving religious leaders and pedophilia comes to light. In 1993 Daniel Eaves, a thirty-six-year-old deacon with the Victory Baptist Church in Springfield, New Jersey, was sentenced to ten years in prison. Eaves pleaded guilty to sexually abusing eight young girls, ages three to fourteen. The sexual offenses occurred at his home and while he chaperoned a youth group from his church. Cornelius Sullivan, the Superior Court judge who sentenced Eaves, stated that the emotional consequences of sexual abuse are so severe that the girls "might have been better off" if Eaves had beaten them with a baseball bat.

Although it would be difficult to name a religion that has not suffered a sexual scandal, the Roman Catholic Church in recent years has grabbed more than its share of unwanted headlines and has paid out over $450 million to settle lawsuits.

On October 5, 1993, James R. Porter, a former Roman Catholic priest, was sentenced to eighteen years in prison after pleading guilty to molesting twenty-eight young boys and girls at three Massachusetts parishes in the 1960s. This was Porter's second conviction on sexual abuse charges. In 1992, long after he retired from the priesthood, Porter served six months in prison for molesting his daughter's teenage baby-sitter at his home.

Victim after victim appeared before the court and told how Porter's abuse caused them to have childhoods fraught with despair. His victims told of horrible nightmares, deep, dark depression, and addictions to drugs and alcohol that lasted long into adulthood.

Some victims were afraid to tell their parents what was happening because Porter threatened harm if they told. Others kept quiet because they were embarrassed and confused; they hated what was happening but it was coming from a man who was next to God. Still others told their parents but were rebuffed because their parents didn't believe the stories. Several parents who did believe their children complained angrily to Porter's superiors. The Catholic Church swept the problem under the rug and simply transferred Porter to a new parish where he continued to molest children.

There are more than 50,000 Catholic priests in the United States. Approximately 1,700 of these priests, or roughly 3.4 percent of the total, are suspected of sexually molesting a child or a teenager.

Once a tightly guarded secret, pedophilia in the priesthood is now out of the closet and the Catholic Church is suffering the worst clerical scandal in modern history.

Increasingly, priests who signed up to serve man and God are now serving time. Father David Holley pleaded guilty to sexually assaulting eight boys and was sentenced to 275 years in prison; he will be eligible for parole in eighteen years. Father Gilbert Goethe, who molested dozens of schoolchildren, plea-bargained for a twenty-year sentence without parole, and Father Myles Patrick White, who filmed himself having sex with boys, is serving four years in hell at the Joliet Correctional Center for his twenty years of sexual abuse.

Thousands of angry victims of pedophilia have stepped forward and forced the Catholic Church to uncircle the wagons and face up to the facts, i.e., thousands of God's children have been hurt, not helped, by going to a priest.

To cure a problem, whether it be alcoholism or pedophilia, one has to first admit that there is a problem. In 1988 the Catholic Church discovered 160 hours of homemade videotapes that showed Father Dino Cinel having sex with teenaged boys. Three years later the Church admitted these tapes were a problem and turned them over to prosecutors. Between 1964 and 1987 there was a problem at Saint Anthony's Seminary, which was a boarding school for aspiring priests in Santa Barbara, California. The problem was that at least twelve priests were playing nude games and having sex with boys ages seven to fourteen. In 1993 the Catholic Church, through Father Joseph Chinnici, finally admitted there was a problem and offered apologies: "The abuses perpetrated by our own brothers on the victims and their families is truly horrific. We totally abhor what has occurred."

When the investigation at Saint Anthony's Seminary began, Father Chinnici did not believe the situation was very serious. "I was wrong," admitted Father Chinnici. "It is not easy, and we acknowledge this terrible truth in a public way because the public trust has been violated. . . ."

But to properly deal with the problem of pedophilia in the priesthood, the public too has to acknowledge a truth. And that truth is that at least 48,300 Catholic priests currently serving in the United States are *not* pedophiles. These priests are serving God; they are helping the children.

Boy Scout Leaders

During the last twenty years the Boy Scouts of America have dismissed approximately 1,800 scoutmasters suspected of sexually molesting boys. Many of these scoutmasters abused dozens of boys on dozens of occasions, in private homes and on camping trips, before being discovered. In several cases Boy Scout leaders dismissed in one state for pedophilic activities were then given new positions with the Boy Scouts of America in another state, where the inappropriate sexual activities continued.

Thomas Hacker, said to be the most outrageously successful child molester ever to infiltrate the Boy Scouts, seduced scores of Scouts for twenty-five years and is now serving a one-hundred-year prison sentence in Illinois. But before being convicted in 1989, Hacker had been fired from one Scout troop in Indiana and then reinstated with a troop in Illinois. He had been forced to resign from three schools after being caught fondling students.

Like many pedophiles, Hacker moved around a lot but always set himself up as a pillar of society in his new community. He was the president of the Holy Name Society, the vice president of the Little League, and was once the director of a municipal agency that ran public parks. One mother was so impressed with Hacker she hired him to tutor her son. The boy later testified that Hacker engaged in sex acts during every tutoring session.

Hacker, who was married and had three sons, abused most of his Scouts during camping trips. Typically, he would visit several boys each night in their tents and zip the flap closed after entering. He often took naked photographs of the boys. This abuse went on for years, despite the fact that other parents were usually on the campouts, sleeping in other tents. Most of his victims apparently kept quiet because of embarrassment, their loyalty to Hacker, and their fear of getting in trouble if anyone knew what they did. Other pedophiles in the Boy Scouts have told their victims to keep quiet about the sex and "to honor the Boy Scout duty of loyalty."

Many of the Scouts reportedly liked Hacker because he allowed them to do things their parents wouldn't, like read *Playboy* magazine and steer his car.

Today many scoutmasters are serving prison sentences for pedophilic activities and the Boy Scouts of America have paid out about $35 million in lawsuits.

Although the Boy Scouts of America have accurately been described as a "magnet for pedophiles," it should be pointed out that more than ninety-seven percent of the organization's 1.15 million adult volunteers are genuinely concerned with your child's welfare. In fact, the Boy Scouts of America have been at the forefront in educating members and volunteers about preventing child molestations. In addition to providing reading materials on the subject to parents and volunteers, the Boy Scouts of America have developed age appropriate educational videos for youths that many believe are the best presentations of their kind. "It Happened to Me" and "A Time to Tell" discuss the warning signs of pedophilia and encourage boys to "yell and tell." All Boy Scout leaders are required to undergo ninety minutes of training in child abuse awareness and prevention.

It is important that parents do not treat the Boy Scouts or any other youth organization as a baby-sitting service. The only way you're going to know who to trust is by *getting involved*. You cannot rely on organizational screening or background checks to weed out pedophiles. Attend meetings, go on camping trips, talk with other parents.

If you cannot go on the overnight camping trips, keep lines of communications open with your son. Ask your child, "How did it go?" "Was it fun?" "Do you want to go on another camping trip?" "Do you like your Scout leader?"

The Boy Scouts of America is an excellent organization that does a huge amount of good. The organization encourages good character and promotes good rules to live by.

One of the best rules established by the Boy Scouts of America in recent years is that all allegations of sexual abuse must be investigated. When an individual is accused of sexual improprieties that individual will be confronted by the Boy Scouts of America and the alleged incident will be reported to the police or to a local child protection agency.

Sexual Abuse in the School

Gregory J. DiFonzo was a popular, award-winning music teacher at Shawmont Elementary School in Philadelphia. In 1993 he was sent to prison for six to twenty years after pleading guilty to sexually abusing a nine-year-old girl in the school music room.

The case began when police, acting on a tip, searched DiFonzo's home and discovered a ten-minute videotape. The tape showed the music room in the school. A nine-year-old student was seated in a chair and the camera zoomed in on her face. DiFonzo's voice could then be heard telling the girl that she had been selected to help make an instructional film that would be viewed by children throughout the city. The purpose of the tape, she was told, was to teach the proper way to play reed instruments and to show how various reeds can be identified by touch or with the tongue. The girl was then blindfolded.

A variety of reeds were then placed in the girl's mouth, and as the demonstration continued, the girl was duped into performing oral sex with her teacher. The sex act continued for ten minutes.

Douglas Marks, a sixty-three-year-old elementary school teacher in Boulder, Montana, was twice voted Teacher of the Year. But this popular teacher was leading a double life; he had been molesting his male students for thirty years. Plying them with money and affection, Marks primarily preyed on young boys from broken homes. Although the school bureaucracy over the years had received many complaints concerning Marks's behavior, he was allowed to practice his pedophilia with impunity. Incredibly, there were actually cases in which he molested male students, watched them grow up, and then molested their sons. Finally, the system, the parents, and the victims could stand no more. After abusing children for three decades, Marks pleaded guilty to sexually assaulting four male students and was given a twenty-year prison term.

Each year in the United States thousands of students are sexually abused in their schools by principals, teachers, coaches, counselors, janitors, and other school employees. This abuse, which frequently includes rape, has taken place in every conceivable location: rest rooms, private offices, storerooms, libraries, hallways, gymnasiums, and classrooms.

Pornographic videotapings of children has become a

common form of sexual abuse in the school environment. Some of the children are tricked into posing in the nude; some are seduced; and some are filmed secretly with hidden cameras. On January 12, 1993, a teacher at the exclusive Phillips Exeter Academy in New Hampshire was convicted of possession and distribution of child pornography. The teacher, Larry Lane Bateman, was dismissed from Exeter after police confiscated 650 pornographic videotapes. In some of the tapes, about ten Exeter students, all males, are shown nude and are engaging in sexual acts. Prosecutors also disclosed that Bateman, the much-admired chairman of the drama department, had set up a video camera and secretly filmed male students in their bathrooms and bedrooms.

Samuel R. Bracigliano, the forty-eight-year-old principal of Gilbert Avenue School in Elmwood Park, New Jersey, was always taking snapshots of his pupils at their elementary school activities. He photographed Christmas and Halloween parties, graduation ceremonies, and other functions and displayed the photos on school bulletin boards. Parents and students alike loved these photographs.

But there were other photos, taken in the privacy of his office, that Mr. Bracigliano did not display.

As so often happens, a casual comment from a child to a parent led to a child abuser's downfall. One boy, who had been invited into Mr. Bracigliano's office, told his father about the funny pictures the principal had taken of him. After the boy talked to his father, the father talked to the police.

Acting on the father's tip, the police obtained a search warrant, raided the principal's home, and seized commercially produced videotapes of naked youths and about fifty photographs of Mr. Bracigliano's students who were posing in provocative positions.

Following an investigation, the principal was also charged with sexually fondling seven of his male students, ages eight through twelve.

Between 1990 and 1994 more than 6,000 children were sexually abused by their coaches and recreational instructors. The victims were enrolled in more than twenty sports including baseball, football, basketball, soccer, swimming, gymnastics, ice skating, wrestling, and dance.

Since the vast majority of coaches are professional and caring, they are naturally embarrassed that a few hundred of their colleagues have been charged with sexual offenses against children.

In San Jose, California, thirty-one-year-old Kerry Lynn Bruton, the ex-president of a youth football league, was convicted of molesting a dozen of his players and sentenced to eighty-two years in prison. In New Jersey Walter S. Bastecki, a baseball coach and president of a Lou Gehrig Baseball League, was found guilty of having sex with six young boys.

Unfortunately, convicting pedophile coaches does not always protect children. When Tracy Kevin Ward, a twenty-four-year-old coach in Prince Georges County, Maryland, was convicted of sexually abusing a twelve-year-old boy, the judge gave him probation and ordered him to stay away from children. But nobody kept an eye on Ward, so he went to a neighboring county and became a wrestling coach. And a baseball coach. And a basketball coach. Ward is now charged with sexually abusing boys on each of those teams.

One pedophile coach secretly filmed his young female

swimmers while they undressed. Another ordered his athletes to show up for individual training, which included a massage and sauna. A third coach was more blatant. "Either participate [in sexual activity] or you are off the team," he told two players.

Teachers and coaches who abuse children usually rely on fear, embarrassment, and intimidation to keep their victims quiet. But some use bribes and other tactics. In Chicago a school principal who was sentenced to a fifteen-year prison term for sexual abuse promised his young victims better grades if they would keep quiet. A third-grade teacher in New York who was caught sexually abusing several of his female students typically sent his victims home with notes excusing them from homework for a week.

Most pedophiles hope that the naivete of their victims will prevent them from fully comprehending what is happening.

After hearing that her daughter's popular fourth-grade teacher and tumbling coach had been arrested for fondling and photographing seven of his female students, one mother was naturally relieved that her daughter's name was not on the list of victims. "I thanked God and breathed a huge sigh of relief," she said.

Now immensely curious about her daughter's teacher, the mother asked, as nonchalantly as possible, "So, Suzie, is your teacher a nice man?"

Without hesitation the little girl responded, "Yeah, he's nice but he thinks I'm a baby or something."

Finding her daughter's response rather odd, the mother asked, "Why do you say that?"

"Because he always feels under my dress to see if I

wet my panties," said the fourth-grader as she playfully skipped out of the room.

"It was the worst moment of my life," said the mother. "Here I've been worried about guns and drugs in the street and my daughter gets abused by her teacher in the safety of a classroom."

Abuse of Very Young Children

At 11:00 P.M., on July 14, 1993, in Gwinnett County, Georgia, a young mother called 911 and reported that her eighteen-month-old daughter "was bleeding from her vagina." Police rushed the child to Henrietta Egleston Hospital for Children.

A caseworker for the Department of Family and Children Services testified in an emergency custody hearing that the child "was torn from her rectum to her vagina" and required several hours of surgery. The caseworker also testified that blond and black pubic hairs were found in the child's genital area, that police discovered bloody diapers at the family's residence, and that a substance believed to be semen was removed from the child's leg . . .

There is evil in the world. And if there is a section of hell reserved for the *most* evil, it will certainly be occupied by the people who sexually abuse infants and toddlers.

Hundreds of infants and toddlers—newborns to four-year-olds—are sexually abused each year by individuals who can only be described as unfathomably disturbed.

In a sampling of 400 cases in which very young children were sexually abused, the author discovered that a little over fifty-five percent were abused by a mother's boyfriend.*

On December 31, 1990, in Milwaukee, Wisconsin, four-year-old Mistydawn Faust was found dead in her mother's apartment. She was bleeding heavily from the groin area. Gary D. Crubaugh, age eighteen, a friend of the little girl's mother, was charged with rape and murder. One week later police and FBI agents launched a search for Kurt Lagoo, an eighteen-month-old boy who had been reported missing. The boy was last seen by his mother's boyfriend who was baby-sitting. While being questioned, the boyfriend admitted that he had killed the boy. An autopsy determined that the boy had been raped. That same year a twenty-one-year-old man in Newark, New Jersey, was charged with the murder of his companion's two-year-old daughter. The girl died of internal bleeding after repeated sexual penetration.

About thirty-five percent of the children abused in this sampling were assaulted by their own fathers, stepfathers, or other relatives. In Lunenburg, Virginia, a twenty-one-month-old boy died while being sodomized. His father was convicted of murder and sentenced to one hundred years in prison.

The rest of the children in this sampling were sexually assaulted by visitors or complete strangers who were in the home on business, renting rooms, or burglarizing the home when the act occurred. In Trenton, New Jersey, a mother awoke and found a thirty-year-old man, who was renting a room, sexually assaulting her two-year-old daughter. The same man had been charged with sexually assaulting a six-year-old girl two years earlier in another house where he was a boarder.

* Although this is not a scientific study the findings are informative.

The most bizarre case occurred in DesPlaines, Illinois, where a forty-nine-year-old investigator with the Illinois Department of Children and Family Services was charged with sexually assaulting a four-month-old girl. The investigator was visiting a friend's home when the child's mother found him lying naked in bed with the child, who was also naked. When the mother began to scream the man fled the scene. Ironically, the investigator was assigned to a unit that checks on day-care centers and foster homes.

Sexual depravity apparently knows no limits and can occur anywhere. On July 12, 1991, a twenty-nine-year-old man raped his three-year-old niece in full view of several rush-hour motorists on the Franklin D. Roosevelt Drive in Manhattan. The man was supposed to be taking the child from the playground to a bathroom but he took her to a grassy area along the highway instead. The man was chased and captured by several passersby who were naturally appalled at what they had witnessed.

Although detailed background information was not available for all 400 cases, a high percentage of the perpetrators had alcohol and drug problems and past records of sexual offenses. At least thirty percent of the young victims were assaulted in middle- to upper-class neighborhoods.

The mother of one victim reported that she knew that the college student renting a room in her attic had some "sexual problems" but said it never occurred to her that someone would "want to have sex with a two-year-old."

We would all like to think that such atrocities are impossible but the reality is that very young children are sexually abused every single day in both rich and poor neighborhoods.

Female Abusers

In Gaithersburg, Maryland, a thirty-nine-year-old woman was charged with statutory rape after admitting to a year-long sexual relationship with a thirteen-year-old boy. The woman, who got pregnant by the teenager, was a friend of the youth's family and initiated the relationship while she was tutoring him with his schoolwork. In 1992 the woman gave birth to a boy and DNA blood tests confirmed that the teenager was the father of the baby. A twenty-four-year-old woman in Fairfax, Virginia, pleaded guilty to statutory rape and was sentenced to thirty days in jail after admitting to a three-year sexual affair with a preteen boy. The woman told police that she and the boy met at a swimming pool where she was the boy's swimming instructor and confessed that the two had sexual relations at least one hundred times. Most of the sex acts occurred at the boy's house while she was allegedly helping him with his schoolwork.

Although pedophiles are overwhelmingly male, the possibility of a female offender should not be overlooked by a concerned parent. More than 2,000 adult women each year are accused of having sexual relations with young children, preteens, and children under fourteen years of age.

A couple dozen cases each year involve a female teacher and young male or female students. On April 16, 1993, in Newport News, Virginia, a judge sentenced Darlene Dudley, a forty-three-year-old English teacher, to three and a half years in prison for having carnal knowledge with a fourteen-year-old student. The judge suspended the sentence but the school fired the teacher and took away her teaching certificate.

In Cambridge, Massachusetts, a thirty-three-year-old female teacher was convicted of raping a fifteen-year-old student after luring him to her home.

Women who sexually abuse young children (three to twelve years old) often do so in tandem with a boyfriend or husband. And as with male pedophiles, women are frequently convicted of incest.

In Washington, D.C., on April 15, 1993, a forty-one-year-old woman pleaded guilty to having sex with her twelve-year-old son and her thirteen-year-old daughter. The following month, in Johnstown, Pennsylvania, a thirty-five-year-old woman was sentenced to ten years in prison for sexually abusing two of her young daughters.

Judges are increasingly giving jail sentences to women who know their children are being sexually abused by a boyfriend or husband but do nothing to stop the activity.

The father of a six-year-old girl who was forced to have oral and digital sex with a twenty-four-year-old female baby-sitter probably spoke for most of us when he stated, "Never in a million years did I think my daughter would be raped by a woman."

Falsely Accused

Being falsely accused of any crime would be horrible. Horrible! Being falsely accused of sexually abusing a child would be the worst nightmare imaginable. Society hates a child molester. Even in violent prison populations, child molesters are considered the lowest form of humanity.

Just imagine. You are going about your life, taking care of your daily duties, and someone says, "He raped my seven-year-old daughter!" or "She molested my little boy!"

People you don't even know are now whispering and pointing fingers as you walk by. Friends and coworkers are suddenly treating you as if you are covered with excrement. Your family is in the limelight and they too have become tainted; they too are feeling the pressure. Money you saved for retirement or a new house is now being spent on legal expenses. Even your supporters are secretly wondering if there is a dark side to you that they have never noticed. You are feeling more anger, rage, and frustration than you have ever felt in your life. You are innocent but your life and reputation have been ruined.

What makes this scene so scary is that it has actually happened to *hundreds* of innocent people.

Sometimes the wrong person is accused of the crime and sometimes a person is accused of a crime that never occurred. A spouse wanting leverage in a custody dispute may accuse his or her partner of abuse. A student angry over a bad grade or angry about being disciplined might get revenge by saying a teacher fondled her. A person looking for a large financial settlement might falsely accuse a priest of misconduct.

It should come as no surprise that there are a lot of people who tell outrageous lies. Some people tell lies for revenge or for some personal gain and others tell lies because they suffer from one of scores of psychological problems.

On May 23, 1993, in Jersey City, New Jersey, a ten-year-old boy told police that he had been kidnapped by a man, tied to a tree, and raped. The boy said that the man called him by his first name and said he knew the boy's mother when he lured him into his car.

Unusually observant, the boy was able to give police a detailed description of his assailant. The man was forty to fifty years old, had a missing tooth, wore an earring, and had a patch of gray in his hair. Police knew a high school cafeteria worker who fit this description exactly and picked him up. Taken to the police station, the boy looked through a one-way glass and identified the man as his attacker. The man was charged with kidnapping, sexual assault on a child, and other charges.

But it was all a lie. The boy eventually recanted his story and admitted that the kidnapping and the rape never occurred. When the police had asked for a description of the assailant the boy had simply described a cafeteria worker at his school.

The child was an incredibly good liar and actor. When the boy was asked to identify the assailant at the police station, he acted just like we would expect a rape victim to act. Seasoned law enforcement officers thought the boy seemed genuinely scared and that his body language and reactions were consistent with someone who had been victimized.

Incredibly, the medical evidence even seemed to confirm the boy's story. A medical examination showed that the boy had a bruised left buttock and a tenderness in his anal area.

Why did the boy lie? We can only speculate. We know that he was a foster child, that he was said to have a low self-esteem, and that he was often picked on at school. Maybe he just wanted attention? Contrary to his parents' wishes, the boy went to an arcade and a Dairy Queen after school. Maybe the boy was looking for an excuse for being late? Although he was not kidnapped or raped, the boy had in fact been tied to a tree by a group of classmates. Maybe the boy was angry about this and figured no one would care unless he blamed an adult and alleged some type of sexual abuse? Discovering that a person lied is often easier than discerning *why* that person lied.

In 1989 David DeJesus was a third-year law student and a caseworker for the New York City Human Resources Administration. On September 19 he was ordered to visit a foster home to investigate allegations of mistreatment.

As the assignment required, DeJesus interviewed a five-year-old foster child privately. Later that day the child allegedly told her foster mother that DeJesus had molested her during the interview.

DeJesus vehemently maintained his innocence but he was arrested for molesting the child and fired from his job. Facing a seven-year prison term and a felony conviction, DeJesus followed his attorney's advice and pleaded "no contest" to a misdemeanor in return for a promise of probation without jail.

A few hours after DeJesus's conviction, the child's biological mother called the prosecutor: the child confessed that her story of molestation was a lie. In a videotaped deposition and again in a hearing, the child explained that her foster mother had forced her to fabricate the story about sexual abuse.

For the next five years DeJesus was forced to fight the courts to get the horrible stain of child molestation off his record. In January 1994, after a painfully slow process, the New York State Supreme Court unanimously overturned DeJesus's conviction "in the interest of justice."

One liar, one phone call, and an innocent man was fired from his job, had his reputation tainted, and faced five years of legal hell. He could easily have gone to jail.

Unfortunately, there are hundreds of these horror stories. In Cambridge, Massachusetts, a seven-year-old girl told police she was kidnapped by a black man on May 2, 1993, taken to a secluded spot, and raped. Police arrested Roger Akankwasa, a twenty-four-year-old college student. Pointing at Akankwasa's photo the seven-year-old girl said, "That's the man who did it." Although all the evidence suggested that Akankwasa could not possibly have been the rapist, he spent thirty-eight days in jail, finally borrowed $15,000 for bail, and waited five agonizing months for his trial.

The night before the trial began the seven-year-old girl recanted her story and sheepishly admitted that she had falsely accused Akankwasa.

Martha Coakley, the Middlesex assistant district attorney in charge of the child abuse unit, was quoted in *The Boston Globe* concerning this case: "I can't think of anything worse than a false claim of child rape."

Actually there is something even worse than being falsely accused of child rape: being falsely convicted!

That is exactly what happened to Kirk Noble Bloodsworth. On July 25, 1984, in Baltimore, Maryland, nine-year-old Dawn Hamilton was raped and murdered. Bloodsworth was convicted of the crime and sent to prison for life. For nine years he sat in prison and screamed, "I didn't do it. I'm innocent."

In 1993 a DNA test concluded that semen found on the victim's panties could not possibly belong to Bloodsworth. After nine years in prison an innocent man was freed.

Increasingly, more and more people accused and convicted of crimes against children are cheering, "Thank God for DNA testing." Through DNA testing, scientists can determine if the genetic material found in semen and blood belongs to the accused. Like a person's fingerprint, everyone has a unique genetic makeup.

Scores of school employees in recent years have been falsely accused of sexually abusing children. In Maryland a twenty-eight-year-old school bus driver was forced to report a thirteen-year-old girl because of her unruly behavior on the bus. In retaliation the girl made up a story that the driver had touched her breast and forced her to touch his penis. At Rochester High School in Michigan a biology teacher lost his job when three girls accused him of fondling their breasts. The teacher was acquitted when the judge learned that two of the girls had lied and the third, under pressure, had exaggerated her testimony. In Compton, California, a high school teacher was accused of having sex with a fifteen-year-old student. The charges were dropped when the girl, under oath, admitted that her story was untrue.

When a group of fourth-grade girls in Illinois decided they did not like their substitute teacher, they did not bother with childish tricks like putting glue on his seat. Instead, one girl offered money to her classmates if they would falsely accuse the teacher of fondling them. The teacher was suspended and probably saw his life passing before him until investigators uncovered the plot.

Unfortunately, being found innocent does not necessarily mean that the accused gets off scot-free. In dozens of cases school employees have had to pay lawyers huge amounts of money to defend them. "I spent over $50,000 proving my innocence," said one employee. "Is that justice?"

Increasingly, the religious community is also vulnerable to false accusations. On November 12, 1993, Steven J. Cook accused Cardinal Joseph Bernardin, one of the nation's most respected Roman Catholic clergymen, of sexually abusing him when he was seventeen years old. The man claimed that Father Bernardin kissed, fondled, and sodomized him. But on February 28, 1994, Cook recanted his story and admitted that his "repressed" memories of the abuse, which arose during and after hypnosis, were unreliable.

Expressing his anger, Cardinal Bernardin said that it was a "travesty" that he, an innocent man and a priest for nearly forty-two years, "was publicly humiliated before the world." It was a "very painful" ordeal, he said.

Many people who claim to have been falsely accused of having sexual activity with children are fighting back in the courts.

On May 13, 1994, in Napa, California, a jury ruled that two therapists ruined a father's life by implanting false memories of child abuse in his daughter's mind.

Former winery executive Gary Ramona had sued two therapists and a hospital, saying their work with his daughter had destroyed his family and cost him his $400,000-a-year job.

After a session in which the sedative sodium amytal was administered, the daughter claimed to have a memory of being raped by her father. The jury apparently believed that the daughter's early medical problems had combined with phantom images and caused unfounded memories. The jurors awarded the father $500,000 in damages.

All accusations of sexual abuse should be taken very seriously and thoroughly investigated. But we also have to remember that some people tell lies, that sometimes mistakes are made, and that in the United States, a person is innocent until proven guilty.

REDUCING THE RISK

- Teach your child that certain parts of his or her body (the area covered by a bathing suit) are private. An adult should not touch them in a private area. Explain the difference between a "good touch" and a "bad touch." Explain that if an adult offers to massage a child's back or feet that could be a "bad touch." Explain that even if it feels good, it is unhealthy for them. Tell your children that an unwanted touch can come from someone you or they know, like, or trust. Children should be instructed to tell parents if anyone touches them in a private area. Tell your children that if someone does touch them inappropriately it is okay to tell Mom and Dad because it is not the child's fault. Use the anatomically correct word for body parts, so children don't learn to be ashamed. Teach children to "yell and tell."

- Children should be told that if an adult asks them to keep a secret from his or her parents, something evil is happening. Encourage children to inform you of anybody or any situation that makes them uncomfortable.

- Empower your children with the right to say no to an adult. When we teach children to be blindly deferential to adults we render them vulnerable to sexual abuse. Teach them to respect their bodies and that they own their bodies. If a child does not want to hug and kiss Uncle Harry, do not force him or her to do so.

- Have frank discussions with older children and teach them the tactics that pedophiles use. Explain that many pedophiles seem like the nicest guys in the world. Tell them to be suspicious if an adult always wants to be alone with them. If an adult is taking photos or providing pornography, gifts, or alcohol, it may be part of a seduction process. Explain that many pedophiles will initiate games and activities that will allow them to touch a child, to spend a night under the same roof, or to see a child undress. Teach children to follow their instincts if they feel something is wrong and not to be blinded by a pedophile's seduction.

- Do not ignore the wolf in sheep's clothing. Eighty percent of all sexual crimes against children are committed by a relative or someone they know. A child molester could be a clergyman, teacher, coach, or baby-sitter. It might also be a stepfather, godfather, or grandfather. The person most likely to sexually abuse a child is the person who spends the most time with that child. Do not underestimate a person (or deny your instincts that something is wrong) simply because that person is in a position of authority or has a friendly demeanor.

- Beware of outside volunteers who are not members of your Boy Scout troop or youth organization. If an organization is desperate for help they may overlook the interviews, background checks, and references that are normally part of a screening process. Many sexual predators use youth groups as hunting grounds.

- Do not use the Boy Scouts, Little League, or religious activities as baby-sitting services. Get involved. Attend meetings. Ask your child open-ended questions about her or his activities. "Do you like the coach?" "Tell me about the weekend, I'm really interested." "Do they treat you well?" Insist on what the Boy Scouts call the "two-deep" policy. The two-deep policy is a rule that at least two adults will be in attendance at youth activities, especially overnights. If your child is going on a group activity, make sure the rest of the group doesn't "cancel." Before automatically giving permission for a child to attend a pajama party, find out who is doing the chaperoning. Is it the mother's new boyfriend?

- Listen to your child. If a child tells you he or she is being molested, believe the child and take action. Too many parents practice denial and ignore children who are reaching out for help. If your child tells you he or she is being touched sexually by someone, your approach should be nurturing, empathic, and nonjudgmental, not accusatory. Make sure the child realizes that it is not his/her fault; the adult is to be blamed, not the child. Be careful that the hostility you feel for the offending adult is not transferred to the child.

- Any child can be seduced by a determined pedophile but the children who are most vulnerable are the children who lack parental affection and love. The most effective prophylactic against child molestation is a loving home where parents are emotionally available and where lines of communication are always open. It is important that your child feels comfortable talking about sensitive issues with you. The child needs you as a parent but also needs you as a best friend.

- Keep an eye out for the warning signs of sexual abuse. Many children who are being molested suffer nightmares and become withdrawn, distracted, moody, or depressed. They may come up with excuses not to go to school or to the place the abuser is located. "I'm sick." Children who are being abused may spend extended periods of time in a fantasy world or may suddenly start soiling themselves. Many abused children lose their appetites, regress to old behaviors like thumb-sucking or bed-wetting, show fear of the dark, or show intense fear of being left with others. Be especially concerned if a child reports itching, pain, bruises, or bleeding in the genital area. It could be a bad sign if a child is suddenly hesitant to undress around you. Many abused children demonstrate an exaggerated knowledge or interest in adult sexual behavior that is expressed in seductive action or conversation. It is normal for children to joke and talk about sex; it is not normal when a nine-year-old talks about or knows how to perform fellatio.

- Hundreds of pedophiles are now making contact with children through computer networks. Since children are often more computer-literate than their parents, it is important that parents ask questions about a child's computer networking and to warn children about inappropriate sexual communications with adults. Ask the child if anyone is sending sexually explicit messages.

■ Child molestation is against the law in every state. If you know or suspect that a child is being abused in any way, report this information to the authorities. Agencies that deal with child abuse are usually listed in the following manner:

> Department of Social Services
> Bureau of Children and Family Services
> Department of Protective Services
> Department of Child Protective Services
> Social and Rehabilitative Services

If you have questions about who to contact and what actions you should take, you could also call ChildHelp USA (1 800 4 A-CHILD) or contact your local police.

3

Firearm Accidents

The incident occurred when I was six years old, but I still remember the deafening explosion, the flames shooting from the muzzle, and the shocking devastation of a .45-caliber bullet. I still remember the horrified look on my mother's face, my father's uncharacteristic anger, and the powerful weapon in my eight-year-old brother's hand.

On that gray winter afternoon my family had been visiting a neighbor, a part-time sheriff. We were gathered in the dining room when the sheriff hoisted a heavy black bag onto the dining-room table. As his wife, my parents, and a number of children gathered together, the sheriff reached into his bag and one by one displayed his treasures. "Guns, real guns. Wow!" I couldn't have been more excited if Santa Claus had offered me a ride in his sleigh and the key to the toy house.

Wide-eyed, I pushed to the front of the adults and watched as my neighbor unloaded the magazine and bullets from a U.S. military, .45-caliber handgun. Lick-ety-split, my brother grabbed the gun in his small hands, screamed, "Bang, bang," and pointed the heavy weapon at an imaginary bad guy in the corner. Still grinning and literally hopping with excitement, he then spun the gun around, aimed it point-blank at my mother's chest, and pulled the trigger. *Click.*

"Never, never, point a gun at someone!" my father shouted. The suddenness of his reaction startled me. I had never seen my father so angry, so emphatic, especially in the presence of neighbors. I felt embarrassed for my brother because the room had grown deathly quiet and everyone was staring at him.

"But, Dad," my brother protested, "the gun isn't loaded, he took the bullets out."

"A gun is always loaded!" my father roared. "Always!" What did he mean, I wondered.

Red-faced and subdued by the interaction, my brother lifted the .45-caliber handgun one more time, pointed at the dining-room wall, and put a little more pressure on the trigger. *BOOM!* The sound was ten times louder than the gunfire I'd heard on television. A bullet from the "unloaded" gun punched through the dining-room wall, careened wildly through the kitchen, and embedded deeply, child high, into the wall next to the basement staircase. Children came rushing up the stairs to investigate the commotion.

The Harsh Reality

Firearm accidents kill an average of 1,500 people each year in the United States and most of the victims are children. And for every person who dies from a firearm accident, ten more are wounded. Thousands of the wounded victims suffer brain and spinal cord injuries that leave them paralyzed, blind, or wheelchair-bound for the rest of their lives. Ironically, the same weapon that is brought home for "protection" is forty times more likely to kill or maim a family member or friend than an intruder.

The stories are always the same, year after year. One child finds the "hidden" shotgun, another child climbs onto a chair and grabs the "unreachable" handgun, and still another pulls the trigger on what he thinks is a toy revolver.

Over and over we hear the same excuses. "I didn't know it was loaded," "I forgot to lock up my gun," "I was just cleaning my handgun," and "We were just horsing around."

In a sense, we've been lucky; the body count could be much higher. More than 100,000 gun owners last year had accidental discharges that crashed through walls, ceilings, furniture, and windows but did not hit any people. Hopefully, these incidents served as a wake-up call for safety.

As a society, we are so satiated with statistics of violence, we often tune out reality. We may listen to the numbers, but we don't hear the screams, see the tears, or feel the heartache. But it is reality that finally smacks us across the face and says, "Wake up." In reality, one second, one senseless accident, and the shooter, the victim, and the parents of both are punished for a lifetime.

The author has recorded and reviewed 31,419 cases (a small percentage of the total incidents) in which children were killed or maimed as a result of firearm accidents. Each accident took one second and each accident caused a lifetime of grief.

Wake up. Don't deny reality. Listen to the screams, see the tears, and feel the heartache:

Los Angeles, California. Tiffany Dailey, four, was shot in the head and killed when her six-year-old sister stumbled upon their father's loaded rifle and somehow pulled the trigger.

Croghan, New York. Kimberly Leaf, five, died after her four-year-old sister found a loaded handgun under her grandmother's mattress, pointed the weapon, and pulled the trigger.

Romulus, Michigan. James Hunt, six, was shot and killed by his three-year-old brother who was playing with an unattended and unsecured shotgun.

Seattle, Washington. A young mother was talking on the phone while her two-year-old son and his three-year-old friend played underfoot. Suddenly the three-year-old spotted a holstered .38-caliber handgun partially hidden beneath a bedroom pillow. The child pulled the pistol from the holster, pulled the trigger, and shot the two-year-old in the stomach.

Billerica, Massachusetts. Ian Sakowich, fourteen, was shot to death by his cousin as the teenagers played with a .25-caliber handgun.

Washington, D.C. Cooper Gibson, three, was fatally shot in the head as he and two siblings played with a handgun in their apartment.

Charlotte, North Carolina. Shoney Gaddy, nine, was shot and killed by his best friend as the two boys played with a shotgun.

Scranton, Pennsylvania. Brandon Smith, six, was shot in the chest and killed by his twelve-year-old brother, who was recklessly loading and unloading a hunting rifle.

Milltown, Wisconsin. Michael Fisk, seven, was accidentally shot in the head and killed by an eleven-year-old boy who was handling a rifle in another room. The bullet passed through a kitchen wall and into the bathroom, where the victim was standing.

I Didn't Know It Was Loaded

Thinking the weapon was unloaded, a fifteen-year-old boy in San Dimas, California, aimed his father's .38-caliber revolver at ten-year-old Josh Smith and pulled the trigger. A bullet from the handgun hit Josh in the head, killing him instantly. On Long Island, New York, a fifteen-year-old boy was showing a .22-caliber handgun to his fourteen-year-old cousin who was seated on a sofa. Thinking the weapon was unloaded, the boy pointed it at his cousin and pulled the trigger. A bullet slammed into the seventh grader's chest and killed him. In Long Beach, California, a fourteen-year-old boy killed his best friend with a shotgun. Joking and pointing the weapon at one another, the boys assumed the powerful shotgun was unloaded. Suddenly there was a huge explosion.

Without a doubt, the deadliest words in the English language are "I didn't know it was loaded." Visualize if you will, the 58,000 names on the Vietnam War Memorial in Washington, D.C.—58,000 names! About the same number of people have been killed or horribly wounded in the United States by "unloaded" firearms. These victims, of course, were not fighting a war in some foreign jungle. They were sitting safely in their living rooms, bedrooms, and basements.

Rule Number One: A FIREARM IS ALWAYS LOADED.

Rule Number Two: NEVER POINT A FIREARM AT SOMEONE IN FUN.

I Was Just Cleaning My Gun

We assume that some safety issues would just be common sense. After all, no reasonable person would jump out of an airplane without a parachute. Only a maniac would drive a car blindfolded. And no one, we assume, would be so irresponsible and negligent to clean a loaded firearm. But we assume too much.

Each year scores of children and adults are maimed or killed by irresponsible gun owners who explain, "I was just cleaning my gun."

The stories are always the same. In Green Bay, Wisconsin, a thirty-year-old father accidentally shot his twenty-two-month-old son to death while cleaning a loaded .22-caliber rifle. A sixteen-year-old Greenbelt, Maryland, youth accidentally killed his thirteen-year-old brother while cleaning his rifle in their bedroom at their mother's apartment.

Many gun owners apparently reason that if they are alone in a room it is not dangerous to attempt to clean a loaded weapon. History proves otherwise. There are two problems with this reasoning. Each year this behavior results in dozens of self-inflicted wounds and deaths and an average of fifty children and adults are wounded or killed each year when bullets pass through ceilings, walls, and windows. In New York a three-week-old boy was shot to death in his crib when a gun his father was cleaning discharged. The bullet tore through a bedroom wall, striking the boy in the chest.

People who attempt to clean a loaded handgun, rifle, or shotgun dramatically increase the chances of killing themselves or someone else.

I Thought the Gun Was Hidden

One five-year-old boy crept into his mother's room, pulled a powerful .44 Magnum handgun from beneath her mattress, and accidentally shot himself in the mouth. The boy's mother had purchased the weapon for protection a week earlier and probably wanted it to be readily accessible. Rummaging through a dresser drawer in his family's Chicago apartment, a four-year-old boy discovered a loaded handgun. While playing with the weapon, the boy killed his three-year-old sister. The .25 caliber bullet entered the girl's left ear and exited the right side of her head. Spotting a handgun in a bedroom closet, a fifteen-year-old boy grabbed the weapon, accidentally pulled the trigger, and killed his best friend.

Never underestimate the lure of a weapon or the ability of a toddler or a teenager to find a handgun, rifle, or shotgun. Children are killed and wounded every day with weapons that parents thought were hidden or out of reach. Hundreds of children have been killed or maimed by firearms "hidden" under beds and beneath mattresses and pillows. Hundreds of children have been killed or maimed by weapons "hidden" in bedside tables and dresser drawers. And hundreds of children have been killed or wounded by firearms "hidden" in unlocked closets and behind couches and other furniture. The facts cannot be denied: mattresses, dresser drawers, and unlocked closets are not proper hiding places for firearms.

Firearms are so pervasive in American society that many owners have developed a cavalier attitude toward safety. In fact, many owners make no effort at all to hide or secure their weapons.

In California a four-year-old boy accidentally shot his three-year-old cousin in the face with a handgun that his father had left on top of a baby stroller. Incidents reported in three other states involve a loaded shotgun left standing in a corner, a handgun left on a bathroom sink, and a weapon left on a kitchen table, all within easy reach of a child's grasp.

Leaving a firearm accessible to a toddler or a teenager is the epitome of parental negligence. Many states have passed laws that will punish these adults. Nevertheless, until owners accept responsibility for their firearms, children will continue to be gunned down like arcade ducks.

To drive home the deadly consequences of children having access to guns, the Alliance for a Greater and Safer Detroit, a concerned citizens group, launched a public service television campaign.

As playful scenes flash across the screen an announcer says: "Give a child a kite and he'll fly it. Give a child a bike and he'll ride it. Give a child some candy and she'll eat it."

The music then turns ominous and somber as the

video shifts to a child slowly approaching a chest of drawers and reaching for a handgun. The announcer then continues, "Give a child a gun . . ."

Viewers then hear the loud bang of a gunshot.

Clowning Around

When guns are combined with horseplay, stunts, pranks, and showing off, tragedy inevitably results. In our sampling of 31,419 firearm accident reports involving children who were killed or wounded almost sixty-five percent included language such as the following:

"We were just clowning around and . . ."

"He was just horsing around . . ."

"She was showing off with her gun . . ."

"We were drinking and passing the revolver around . . ."

"He was reenacting a scene from the movie . . ."

"He was twirling the gun on his finger and . . ."

"I was kidding around, just trying to scare her . . ."

"She was laughing and passing her gun around . . ."

"We were playing quick draw and . . ."

Years ago, teachers disciplined children by making them write their offense over and over again on the blackboard. "I will not pull Becky's pigtail." "I will not pull Becky's pigtail." Today, when offenses are more serious ("I will not shoot Becky." "I will not sell Becky drugs.") this punishment would probably be considered antiquated and laughable. Nevertheless, the one message we need to repeat a thousand times if necessary is "Don't Clown Around with Guns." "Don't Clown Around with Guns." "Don't Clown Around with Guns . . ."

Pistols and Parties

Increasingly, teenagers and younger children are bringing pistols to parties with tragic results. In recent years, over one hundred cases have been reported in which children have been wounded or killed when firearms discharged at slumber parties, birthday parties, and other parties.

Tony Hall, a twelve-year-old junior high school student in Anchorage, Alaska, was shot in the chest and killed by a fourteen-year-old friend who brought his parents' powerful .357 handgun to a slumber party. In New York thirteen-year-old Sabrina Williams (nicknamed "Smurf" because she was so friendly and outgoing) was dancing in the living room at her sister's birthday party when she was shot in the head and killed. Her fourteen-year-old brother was playing with a handgun he thought was unloaded when it discharged accidentally. On February 28, 1994, in Philadelphia, thirteen-year-old Wilfredo Lopez, handsome, clean-cut, and a good student, ruined his own life and ended the life of a friend. Young Wilfredo was attending a neighborhood girl's "Sweet Sixteen" party and began playing with a .25-caliber handgun that was being passed around. The weapon discharged and hit his friend, thirteen-year-old Danny Santana, dead center in the heart. Wilfredo, a former altar boy, was charged with murder and wishes the weapon had never been brought to the party.

Usually overshadowed by the presence of alcohol and drugs, pistols at parties are a reality that parents must address. Like adults, children respond well to facts. Communicate to them that pistols and parties do not mix. Explain that Tony Hall, Sabrina Williams, Danny Santana, and scores of other children are dead because some jerk brought a handgun to a party. Explain that when a child gets wounded or killed, many lives are ruined—those of the victim, the shooter, and their family members. Encourage children to refuse to participate if a weapon is produced at a party, to notify an adult, and to leave. Teach children and teens that firearms are not toys; nor are they "cool." Finally, set an example by keeping weapons out of the hands of your own children.

Russian Roulette

The powerful .357 Magnum revolver, taken from his father's closet, made the fifteen-year-old high school sophomore feel important, made him feel tough, so he showed it to two of his classmates in the basement of his home. Seeing that they were duly impressed, the teenager loaded the six-shot weapon with one bullet, spun the cylinder, and pointed the barrel to his right temple.

"Let's play Russian roulette," said the teenager. Not wanting to appear afraid, neither of the classmates ob-

jected. The teenager closed his eyes and slowly pulled
back the trigger until the hammer slammed forward.
Click. "Oh, man, you're crazy," shouted one of the
classmates approvingly. The other classmate just
laughed.

Basking in the attention, the tenth-grader spun the
cylinder one more time, grinned at his buddies, and
again placed the barrel to his right temple. Secretly, he
hoped the story would get around at school and that he
would gain a reputation as a macho and daring guy.
Once again he smiled at his friends, closed his eyes, and
slowly squeezed the trigger. *BOOM!* The bullet exited
his left temple. He was dead before his body hit the
ground. . . .

Reginald Davey, Michael Orr, Jorge Ortega, Michael
Jackson, Raymond Winchester, John Thomas, and at
least 194 other teenagers have all died in recent years
playing Russian roulette.

Close your eyes and visualize nearly 200 dead teenagers. Visualize 200 funerals. Focus on the senselessness
and the wasted lives.

Russian roulette is a deadly dare. Don't do it.

Accidents Outside the Home

It should be pointed out that not all firearm accidents
involving toddlers occur in the home; young children
have also discovered and fired weapons in cars, schools,
offices, and even stores. In Miami, Florida, a three-year-
old girl accidentally shot and killed a twenty-eight-year-
old woman who was paying for merchandise in a conve-
nience store. The toddler came into the store with her
grandfather about 1:00 P.M. and discovered a handgun

kept behind the counter for protection. Playing with the gun, the little girl pulled the trigger. A bullet passed through the counter into the customer.

With the increase in carjackings and other highly publicized highway crimes, more and more adults are carrying firearms in their cars for protection. As would be expected, the number of firearm accidents in cars is increasing. In Port Arthur, Texas, a fourteen-month-old boy was left unattended in a parked car with his three-year-old sister while their mother shopped in a nearby food store. The little girl discovered a .25-caliber handgun that belonged to her mother and began playing with it. Suddenly there was a loud bang and the fourteen-month-old boy was dead from a gunshot wound to his head.

Most people would assume they would be safe from firearm accidents in a church parking lot. Most people assume they won't be killed by a three-year-old. But when you combine a loaded weapon, an irresponsible adult, and a child, tragedy can occur anywhere.

Wayne Johnson, his wife, and their three-year-old son had just attended a service at the Lexington Baptist church in Virginia and were climbing into the family pickup truck. As the little boy scrambled into the vehicle, he either jostled or grabbed the trigger of his father's loaded shotgun, which was proudly displayed in a rack across the back window. The shotgun discharged with a deafening explosion, sending a twelve-gauge slug into a car parked twelve feet away. Linda Myers, the deacon's wife, was killed instantly. Why was it necessary to bring a deer hunting weapon to church? Why was it loaded, chambered, and off safe?

Astoundingly, many adults apparently believe that a child is incapable of picking up a gun and pulling a trigger. Nothing could be further from the truth! Hundreds of children, many under the age of five (and some as young as fifteen months), have picked up handguns, rifles, and shotguns and accidentally shot themselves, other children, or adults.

REDUCING THE RISK

- Firearm accidents this year will kill 1,500 people in the United States and will seriously injure 10,000 others. One senseless mistake and the shooter, the victim, and their families will be punished for a lifetime. Face up to the reality of firearm accidents and refuse to be a statistic. Be pro safety.

- Before you bring a gun into the home for protection carefully evaluate your own situation and weigh the potential risks with the benefits. Is there a heavy drinker in the house? Is there an abusive spouse? Are young children present? Does someone in the home suffer from depression? Are your teenagers responsible and mature? Make sure that a weapon brought into the home for "protection" doesn't kill the people it was supposed to protect.

- Take a firearm safety course that includes live firing. But don't get overconfident! As with any skill, one does not become an expert with only three or even one hundred hours of training. The author has had over 1,000 hours of training but still has much to learn about firearms. Training means that you recognize the irreversibility of pulling the trigger. It means you don't risk the lives of innocent bystanders. It means you don't shoot until you are sure of your target. Scores of people have fired at noises in the night and ended up killing their loved ones.

■ "I didn't know it was loaded" are the deadliest words in the English language. Treat every handgun, rifle, and shotgun as if it is loaded. Never point a weapon at someone in fun. Never!

■ When guns are combined with horseplay, stunts, and pranks the result is always the same: TRAGEDY. Bluntly stated, anyone who shows off and clowns around with a firearm is an ass and a fool. In thousands of recorded cases he/she is also a murderer.

■ When you clean a weapon make sure it is unloaded and pointed away from people. And remember, at least fifty people are wounded and killed each year when bullets are accidentally fired through ceilings, walls, and windows.

■ Never underestimate the lure of a gun or the ability of a toddler or teenager (or criminal) to find your weapon. Thousands of children have been accidentally wounded or killed after finding weapons in dresser drawers, unlocked closets, and beneath pillows or mattresses. Thousands! Quick access for self-defense also means quick access for a child. Weigh the risks and the benefits.

■ Where children are present, weapons should be unloaded, fitted with a trigger-locking device, and hidden in a locked closet or cabinet. Make sure the keys are also inaccessible.

- If a weapon is displayed at a party, tell an adult and leave immediately. (And why not leave, you are in the company of a total jerk.) A weapon that is being passed around is a red flag to danger; never participate. The mature person understands what a gun can do. Losers show off guns at parties. Winners and true warriors never allow a loser to endanger their lives.

- Toddlers are fully capable of finding a gun, picking it up, and pulling a trigger. Many children as young as fifteen months have accidentally killed themselves and other children. It is the responsibility of adults to recognize this reality and to separate children from firearms. Toy guns today look very much like real guns. "Bang, bang, you're dead" is often more than just a game.

- Teach children the five basic rules if they come across a gun:

Stop.

Don't Touch.

Leave the Area.

Tell an Adult.

Guns Are Not Toys.

4

Household Accidents

Children die every day in household accidents. Some are electrocuted, burned, or scalded. Some die from falls or from falling furniture and appliances. And some children are run over in their own driveways or die after ingesting drugs, cleaning solvents, and other poisons.

In Brooklyn, New York, a four-year-old boy was killed when a large television toppled over on him. Apparently, the twenty-seven-inch Magnavox fell from a wheeled cart as the boy pulled or pushed the television in his family's living room. His mother and aunt heard a loud cry, rushed into the living room, and found the boy pinned beneath the set. In New Haven, Connecticut, an eighteen-month-old boy died of alcohol poisoning after swallowing four ounces of Scotch. The child grabbed the cup from a low table, gulped down the drink, and was pronounced dead at 3:00 A.M. at Yale–New Haven Hospital.

The author has reviewed nearly 1,300 fatal and near-fatal household accidents involving children. These accidents occurred in lower-, middle-, and upper-income homes. Although some parents and baby-sitters of the victims were clearly negligent, most were loving and otherwise conscientious people who simply were not aware of the potential dangers. As imperfect humans we all make mistakes and we all have a lot to learn about safety.

"Household Accidents" is designed to help us learn from other people's mistakes and to increase our safety awareness. The father of a two-year-old girl who died after drinking a pesticide told the author, "We can't bring our daughter back—but we can share our lesson and hopefully save the lives of other children."

Poisons

Young children explore their worlds with hands and mouth. Propelled by curiosity, children have developed a rather simplistic philosophy of life: they touch, taste, and eat everything they see.

To an adult, a collection of cleaners, paints, and pesticides is an environmental eyesore. But an infant or toddler views the same collection as a banquet. Store this potpourri of poisons at ground level and our crawling connoisseurs will assume it is a picnic.

Poisoning is the most common household accident for children under six years of age. It is also one of the most lethal. Every year, more than one million parents and baby-sitters call poison control centers, frantically requesting information. "My baby has just swallowed some . . ." is repeated 20,000 times per year in each of our fifty states.

An average of fifty children die every year in the United States after ingesting oven and drain cleaners, pesticides, weed killers, paint removers, bleach, kerosene, antifreeze, floor polish, and many other products, including cosmetics, prescription drugs, and alcohol. Thousands of other children survive their encounters with these poisons but suffer serious burns and illnesses that require hospitalization.

According to the American Association of Poison Control Centers, between 1986 and 1993 at least forty children died after eating iron supplement pills. Many of these pills were not in child-resistant bottles. It is assumed that the young victims saw their mothers taking these pills and probably thought the pills were candy.

Candy-flavored medicine and vitamins are another problem. In fact, overdoses of good-tasting baby aspirin and vitamins are one of the leading causes of poisoning in young children. When children believe these products are candy, they will make every effort to get them.

A four-year-old girl in New York City died after drinking her father's methadone, which he stored in a Gatorade bottle in the refrigerator. Methadone is prescribed to drug addicts as a substitute for heroin and has been responsible for several child poisonings. In other cases a four-year-old girl drank paint remover that her father had placed on the porch in a soft drink can and a three-year-old boy died after eating dozens of antidepressant pills belonging to his mother.

Tragically, there are dozens of cases in which loving parents have accidentally poisoned their own children. This usually occurs when a prescription drug or other product is stored in some innocuous-looking container. Forgetting that she had stored her own prescription in an empty aspirin bottle, one mother inadvertently fed

powerful tranquilizers to her feverish four-year-old
daughter. In another case a baby-sitter sprinkled white
roach killer on a child's cereal because someone had
stored the poison in a box marked "sugar."

Thousands of poisoning emergencies could be prevented each year if proper precautions were taken with
prescription drugs, cleaning agents, and other potentially harmful products. Since children will continue to
"touch, taste, and eat everything they see," our policy
concerning dangerous products in the home should be
"out of sight, out of reach, and locked away." This is a
policy that will save lives.

Falling Furniture

A two-year-old boy in Monroe, Connecticut, was
killed when a bedroom dresser fell on top of him. The
boy's mother put the victim and his twin brother down
for a nap and left the bedroom to do some housework.
When she returned a short time later to check on the
twins, she found one son beneath the dresser, unconscious. Apparently the twins had been playing and managed to open the dresser drawers, even though devices
had been installed to keep them closed. The dresser fell
over and the little boy died of traumatic asphyxia, or
lack of oxygen.

Scores of children have been killed and hundreds
have been seriously injured when dressers, bookcases,
televisions, microwaves, file cabinets, and other furniture and appliances fell on top of them.

Falling furniture and appliances pose a very real and
serious danger to children. Toddlers and young children
often grab ahold of bookcases to pull themselves into

standing positions. They love to climb on chairs and reach on top of dressers and tables for little treasures. Children are always climbing on or bumping into appliances and furniture.

To analyze the risk of falling furniture in your own home, it is important to understand that there are many different types of accidents.

Pretending he was piloting a rocket ship, a four-year-old boy was tearing through his father's study on a three-wheeled low rider (sort of a cross between a tricycle and the space shuttle) when the oversize front wheel collided with the leg of a collapsible metal computer table. The table buckled and like meteorites, a computer, a word processor, and a printer crashed loudly to earth. The future astronaut survived his first gravity lesson unscathed, but his father's expensive equipment was unsalvageable. Today, three deep craters in the hard wooden floor stand as reminders of what could have been a serious injury to a child.

Hundreds of other children have been less fortunate. One seven-year old was crushed when his father's heavy tool cabinet fell from a workbench and pinned him against the hood of a car in the family's garage. The child was standing on the car's front bumper reaching for a hammer on the top shelf of the cabinet when it toppled over.

A brother and sister, ages three and four, were seriously injured when one of them was either reaching for a book or climbing onto a seven-foot-high bookcase. The bookcase, containing heavy law books, fell on the two children. Both children were hospitalized with multiple broken bones.

There are many scenarios to consider. After changing a bulb in a ceiling light, one man apparently failed to secure the decorative glass cover properly. Later, when his son slammed a door, the cover jarred loose from the ceiling and hit the boy in the head, resulting in a concussion and over one hundred stitches. In order to vacuum her living-room rug, a thirty-year-old woman piled an end table, chairs, and other furniture on top of a large desk to get them out of the way. While she manipulated the noisy vacuum cleaner, the woman's young daughter pulled the precariously piled furniture down on top of her. A fatal accident occurred in the home of a couple who were redecorating their recreation room. Workmen had delivered a 300-pound ceiling-to-floor mirror and leaned it against a sofa. Before it could be mounted on the wall, their three-year-old boy gave it a tug.

Parents should conduct safety surveys of their own homes. What are the chances that a heavy television, stereo, microwave, or lamp could fall or be pulled off a table? Does that table have weak or collapsible legs? Tall, top-heavy pieces of furniture like bookcases (a real problem) should be secured to a wall at the highest level with wire or nails. If a child trips on an extension cord (a danger in itself), will a heavy lamp be yanked off a table? If two drawers in your dresser are opened simultaneously, will the dresser topple over? What objects in the garage pose a danger to children? How about closets?

In truth, some accidents will occur no matter how many precautions are taken. But ninety percent of the so-called "falling furniture" accidents are absolutely preventable.

Driveways

Before kindergarten and before we were allowed to venture out of our own yards there was the sanctity of the driveway. Any child who had a driveway at his or her home knew the rules: "Okay, you can play in the driveway, but don't go into the street." We would have preferred the street, of course, but anything was better than being cooped up in the house when all the television channels were cluttered with news. Driveways, we came to realize, were where children played; adults played in the street.

But it appears that many adults forget that they have granted their children free reign of the driveway. During the last decade more than 1,200 kids have been run over while playing in their driveways. A three-year-old girl in Reston, Virginia, was run over and killed in her driveway when her father moved his pickup truck. In Anchorage, Alaska, a twenty-seven-year-old woman chugged a couple of rum and Cokes, started up her car, and killed a three-year-old girl who was playing in her driveway. In other sad cases a seventy-year-old woman ran over her eighteen-month-old grandson; a teenager, who had just gotten her license, backed over her four-year-old brother. Both victims were playing with toys in the driveways of their homes.

A high percentage of driveway accidents occur when friends and family members are saying good-bye to one another following a get-together. Typically, there is a lot of hugging and kissing, several people are talking at once, and a child wanders by unnoticed by a driver who is busy waving to a group on the front porch as he backs out of the driveway.

Few people will be surprised to hear that hundreds of

driveway accidents have involved alcohol. A number of inebriated drivers have even unknowingly backed over children riding tricycles. One woman, who had almost three times the legal blood alcohol content, ran over and killed a three-year-old neighbor who was playing with dolls in the driveway. Not realizing what she had done, the woman continued on into town where she casually filled out an application for a job.

In several driveway accidents, motorists put the car in drive when they intended to put it in reverse (or vice versa), and subsequently pinned children against garage doors. In other cases drivers have forgotten to set their emergency brakes, with tragic results.

Some of the children who have been killed in driveways have been hit by strangers: taxi drivers, garbage truck drivers, and motorists using available driveways to turn around. But as might be expected, most driveway accidents involve a friend or a relative. This, of course, adds to an already horrible tragedy.

In many cases obstacles have obscured the vision of the driver. On May 11, 1994, in Bridgewater, Massachusetts, a man returning home from work did not see his six-year-old son and a friend playing in the driveway and ran over them both, killing his son. The man's view was obscured by a mailbox, bushes, and a shade tree under which the boys were resting.

REDUCING THE RISK

POISONS

■ Remember, to an adult a box of polishes, paints, and pesticides is an unsightly but necessary evil. But a curious and hungry toddler sees this same box and is happier than a connoisseur at a wine-tasting party. Store all poisonous cleaners, pesticides, and medicines *out of sight, out of reach, and preferably in a locked cabinet.* Poisons stored beneath the kitchen sink are *not* out of sight or out of reach. This year thousands of children will be poisoned by products they discover in bathrooms, kitchens, garages, and outdoor storage areas. Do not underestimate a child's ability to gct at poisonous tasty delights.

- Post the number of your local poison control center near your phonc. In thc cvent of a poisoning, time is extremely important. Tell your baby-sitter about this number. Keep syrup of ipecac in your home, but never givc it to a child without first calling the poison control center or your doctor.

- When you use a medicine or a household cleaner, put it away immediately. It only takes a moment for a child to discover a dangerous product and it only takes one taste to poison a child. Put the product away before answering the phone or a knock at the door.

- The most dangerous household products include oven and drain cleaners, weed killers, metal polish, kerosene and lighter fluid, paint solvents, antifreeze, bleach, prescription and illegal drugs, and nonprescription legal drugs. Simple, easily installed safcty latchcs arc available for drawers and cabinets that contain medicines or poisonous household products.

- Don't underestimate the dangerous potential of perfumes, cosmetics, vitamins, mouthwash, aspirins, or alcoholic drinks left unattended. Remember, hundreds of products like after-shave lotion, deodorizer cakes, and Fido's flea powder have all caused poisonings.

■ It is dangerous to encourage your child to take medicine by telling him/her it is "candy." Children might search for this "candy" and swallow a lethal dosage. Don't deceive your children. They should be taught to respect medicine as something that will help them if they are sick.

■ Dangerous substances should be stored away from food. Do not transfer harmful substances into innocuous-looking containers like soda cans, milk cartons, bowls, jars, cookie tins, or boxes marked "sugar." Be extremely careful about what you store in the refrigerator.

■ Prescription drugs should be stored in properly labeled, child-resistant containers. It is very dangerous to store tranquilizers, iron pills, or other drugs in empty aspirin bottles or other innocent-looking containers. Clean out medicine cabinets every six months and dispose of old medicines. Purchase products that are in safety containers. Do not administer or ingest medicines in the dark.

FALLING FURNITURE

■ Falling furniture and appliances pose a very real and serious danger for children. Scores of children have been killed and hundreds have been seriously injured when bookcases, dressers, televisions, and other heavy objects have fallen on them.

- Conduct a safety survey of your home. Make sure that tall, top-heavy bookcases are secured to the wall. If a child opens all the drawers in a dresser or file cabinet, is it likely to fall? Safety latches are available that will prevent drawers from being opened by a child. Safe dressers and file cabinets are designed so that only one drawer can be opened at a time. Will a slammed door or heavy wind jar heavy objects from your ceiling or walls? Do you have heavy objects stored on a table that has weak or collapsible legs? Make sure any heavy objects hanging on walls, including framed pictures, are properly secured and that tables are sturdy enough to withstand the impact of a speeding child.

- Statistically, garages have become particularly dangerous. Children have been killed or seriously injured when heavy ladders, tool cabinets, and shelves have collapsed on top of them.

- Mirrors and glass tables are very beautiful but can also be very dangerous when children crawl, stand, fly, or crash into them.

- Be especially careful when you are renovating or moving in or out of your home; there is much confusion and many heavy boxes, boards, and pieces of furniture that could harm a child.

DRIVEWAYS

■ During the last decade more than 1,200 children have been run over while playing in driveways. Enter and exit driveways very slowly. Before departing, WALK around your car and inspect for children.

■ Clear away bushes, piles of leaves, and other obstacles that might obscure a driver's vision.

■ Be especially careful during holiday get-togethers and other functions when many people are saying good-bye in the driveway. In the confusion a child might crawl under or behind a car.

■ When parking in a driveway be sure to set your emergency brake, put your car in park, take your keys out of the ignition, and lock your doors.

■ Warming up your car in the driveway can be dangerous if the vehicle is left unattended. In some cases vehicles have slipped into gear and lunged forward or backward. In other cases children have put cars into gear. It should also be noted that over 400 vehicles are stolen each year while they are being "warmed up."

■ The most dangerous monster children have to fear is the drunk driver. If you drink, don't drive.

■ Test your garage door opener. At least fifty-five young children and teenagers have been killed when they got caught under automatic garage doors. Others suffered brain damage or other serious injuries.

To check the unit's reversing mechanism, place a thick piece of wood on the garage floor in the door's path and then press the control button. The garage door should reverse immediately after striking the wood. If not, disassemble the unit until repairs can be made. Units built before 1982 are least likely to have auto-reversing features. It is important to know where the emergency-release mechanism is located.

GENERAL TIPS

- We were warned when we were children and it's still true: children frequently suffocate in discarded refrigerators, freezers, ice chests, and other airtight containers. When you dispose of an old refrigerator or like item, you have a number of options: (1) Remove the door (2) Drill airholes in the container (3) Remove the door latch so that the door cannot close or lock (4) Attach a locking device so that the container cannot be opened and crawled into (5) Cart that old eyesore to the junkyard.

- Purchase and install smoke detectors. Test them once a month and replace the batteries at least once a year. Without exaggeration, smoke detectors have saved the lives of *thousands* of children. Practice two escape routes from your home and teach your children what to do in the event of a fire. Make sure your children know to dial 911 in emergency situations and that they know their address.

- Prevent falls in your home by never leaving babies alone on furniture. Strap children into high chairs and use safety gates on stairs. (Safety gates should not have openings or tops that could catch a child's head or neck.) Many infants fall off tables while being changed. Before diapering, gather the things you will need. If you forget something, keep one hand on the baby or take the baby with you while you get it. Never leave your baby unguarded on anything from which he or she might fall.

■ Keep all plastic bags and wrapping materials, such as dry cleaning, produce, or trash bags, away from children. Many children have suffocated when plastic bags covered their heads or faces. Never use thin plastic material to cover mattresses or pillows—the plastic might cling to an infant's face, causing suffocation.

■ Scores of children are burned each year by hot liquids their parents are holding. Put your coffee down before you pick up or hold a child. When cooking, it is a good idea to use the back burners of the stove; front burners can be easily touched by children. Always turn handles of cooking pots toward the back of the stove. Keep containers of hot food in the center of the table where they are more difficult to reach. Do not allow children to crawl around the kitchen while you are cooking or serving meals. In 1993 more than 220 children were stepped on, burned, or injured by dropped knives and other objects while one of their parents was cooking in the kitchen.

■ Hundreds of children have been scalded when they carelessly opened packages taken from a microwave. Children should be taught to follow food-label instructions and to open containers away from themselves. If children are too young to read, they are too young to use a microwave.

- Install safety plugs or covers on all unused wall sockets within reach of children. These will prevent children from sticking fingers and other objects into those intriguing little holes.

- Many hand-me-down older cribs are considered unsafe. To prevent strangulation the space between the crib bars should be no wider than 2¼ inches. The headboard should be rounded and smooth with no corner posts sticking up. There should be nothing on the headboard that a neck or wrist could get caught in. The mattress should fit snugly against the sides of the crib. Children have suffocated and received other injuries when their faces or limbs lodged between the open space between the mattress and the sides of the crib. If the mattress is not flush with the sides of the crib, fill the extra space with rolled towels. Use a waterproof mattress pad, *not a plastic bag*, to protect the mattress. Make sure there are no electric cords, drapery, or venetian blind cords near your child's crib or playpen. Hanging crib toys and mobiles should be kept out of your child's reach. Don't hang laundry bags or anything with strings on the crib. Make sure there are no electrical outlets within reach. If your child can push up, remove bumpers and toys from the crib. A child might use these to climb out of the crib and suffer a fall. Mesh playpens and portable cribs should never be used with a side left down; the mesh forms a loose pocket into which an infant could roll and suffocate.

■ Recognize the dangers of carbon monoxide poisoning. On July 2, 1994, in West Palm Beach, Florida, five people, including two children, were found dead inside a house after someone left a van running in the garage. Never leave a vehicle running in an enclosed area. Carbon monoxide poisoning has killed hundreds of people.

■ Soft bedding suffocates 1,800 infants each year. A two-year study by the Consumer Product Safety Commission found that up to 30 percent of the 6,000 annual cases of sudden infant death syndrome (SIDS) were the result of placing a baby on top of soft bedding such as pillows, comforters and sheepskins. SIDS is the death, for no apparent cause, of babies younger than one year old. Researchers believe the infants' bedding covers their mouths and noses, and they die of carbon dioxide poisoning as a result of breathing the trapped air they have exhaled. Never put a baby to rest on top of fluffy bedclothes or soft bedding. Most experts advise that babies be put to sleep on their backs or sides.

■ Zippered beanbag chairs can be dangerous. On December 1, 1994, the Consumer Product Safety Commission recalled ten million zippered beanbag chairs because they are hazardous to children. At least five children have died after inhaling or ingesting some of the beanbag fillings. In Unionville, Missouri, a 19-month-old boy died when he unzipped a chair, crawled inside and suffocated from inhaling the foam pellet filling. Other children have choked while playing with the pellets outside of the bag. Consumers should stop using any beanbag chairs with zippers and take them away from children. The CPSC can be contacted for repair instructions and additional information at 1-800-638-2772.

■ Many bunk beds are unsafe. During May 1995 the Consumer Product Safety Commission recalled more than 320,000 wooden bunk beds produced by eleven manufacturers because of potentially hazardous spaces in the headboards and footboards of the top bunks. The CPSC stated that parents should stop putting young children to sleep in bunk beds with frame and guardrail openings larger than 3.5 inches because the youngsters could strangle trying to crawl through the openings. Twenty-five children died in bunk beds from 1990 to 1995 after they wiggled throught the guardrail, only to be left dangling by the neck because their heads were too big to pass through. Openings between the mattress and frame, and between the bed and a wall, pose additional strangulation hazards. Consumers should examine bunk beds in their homes, measure spaces and check for the manufacturer's name. If the spaces are larger than 3.5 inches, they should call the CPSC toll-free at 1-800-638-2772 or contact the retailer or manufacturer about getting repair material.

■ Water beds pose special risks for young children. On September 1, 1994, a three-month-old girl in Pennsylvania became the sixth child to die while sleeping on a water bed. Authorities believe that the soft nature of the water bed causes children to inhale their own exhaled breath. The children die because the carbon dioxide becomes pocketed around their faces.

5

Windows

Falling Out of Windows

In 1991 Conor Clapton, the young son of rock guitarist Eric Clapton, was killed after falling from a high-rise apartment window in New York. Left alone for just one minute, the curious child crawled over to the unprotected opening and fell fifty-three floors to his death.

Sadly, young Conor is just one of nearly one hundred children to be killed each year by falling out of windows. Thousands of other children suffer spinal cord and neck injuries, fractured skulls, multiple broken bones, and other serious injuries.

Following his son's accident, Eric Clapton wrote his award-winning "Tears from Heaven" and dedicated it to Conor's memory. Clapton has also done public service announcements to make people aware that windows can be dangerous for children. He urges parents to take safety precautions against such risks.

"I worried that Jimmy would run into the street or be kidnapped," said a young mother whose son broke his neck after falling from a town-house window. "The danger of windows never even occurred to me."

Unfortunately, the dangers often do not occur to most parents until it is too late. But the dangers are real. In Chicago five-year-old Jeffrey Moman and two-year-olds Maurice Britton and Troy Kirk all fell to their deaths after pushing through screens or playing near unprotected windows in their high-rise apartments. In Boston twenty-one-month-old Iris Negron and three-year-old Willie Graham both plunged to their deaths. Willie was reportedly jumping on his bed and somehow bounced out the window. Four-year-old Terrell Smith of Philadelphia and five-year-old Darryl Napper of Washington, D.C., also died when they leaned too far out of unprotected apartment windows.

Since young children tend to be top-heavy (their heads are big compared to their bodies), most will land on their heads when they fall out of a window, making even short falls dangerous. Naturally, the tendency to land on their heads increases the chances that children will suffer severe brain injury or death. The good news is that when children fall, they are more relaxed than adults and are less likely to break bones.

The Hand of God

Sometimes we get lucky. Sometimes there is a miracle. In Southfield, Michigan, Gina Beatty diapered her two-year-old son Joshua and put him down for a nap after his noontime meal. Apparently not ready to sleep, little Joshua got out of bed and crawled over to his ninth-floor bedroom window. As Joshua leaned against the aluminum frame, he accidentally pushed out the screen and fell out the window.

Joshua tumbled about ninety feet before landing in a bush that snagged his diaper, stripped him naked, and saved his life.

When the building manager arrived, huffing and puffing, in the lobby, he noticed a diaper dangling in the bush and found Joshua standing there naked with leaves on his chest. His only injury was a scratch on his forehead.

"What happened?" asked the manager.

"I f-f-fell," Joshua stammered.

Quoted in the Baltimore *Sun*, Lonnie Thompson, a maintenance worker at the Charter House Apartments, stated, "It was like God held out his hands and caught him."

Miracles do happen. Medical experts in New York are still hard-pressed to explain how five-year-old Paul Rosen could fall seven stories from his parents' Upper East Side apartment, land on his rear end on a concrete courtyard, and escape with only a few minor bruises.

Paul was reaching for a toy suspended by a string from his bedroom window when he fell. Seeing what happened, Paul's father bolted down the stairs in a panic, screaming his son's name. Expecting the worst, Mr. Rosen found his son sitting down, looking bewildered, but okay. When emergency medical technicians arrived, the little boy reportedly wanted to know if he would get a Band-Aid.

Raymond Bonner, a medical technician who rushed

to the scene, told the *Daily News,* "It was like the angels caught him."

A toddler in Hong Kong who plunged nineteen floors from a high-rise apartment window may well hold the world's survival record.

Three-year-old Fong Kong-hei was reaching out the bathroom window trying to collect socks from a clothesline when he fell and fell and fell. Fortunately, the tot's fall was broken on the way down by other clotheslines before he landed in a flower garden. The boy was knocked unconscious, but made a full recovery.

God does indeed work in strange ways. On June 22, 1994, in Camden, New Jersey, two-year-old Matthew Mikels picked up his cat and, still clutching his cuddly pet, somehow stumbled out a third-floor apartment window. As the two tumbled past lower balconies the cat landed first and Matthew landed on top of it. Matthew suffered a broken arm but survived; the cat that cushioned his fall utilized the last of his nine lives for a very good cause.

Great Catches

Six-year-old Javon Saucier of New Haven, Connecticut, was playing football when he made a twenty-yard dash and made the most important reception of his young life: catching a three-year-old neighbor falling from a window.

It all started when Brandon Ellison's mother told him he couldn't go out to play. Frustrated with his sentence, the three-year-old decided to escape through a second-floor window, sixteen feet off the ground. Hanging from the window ledge, Brandon apparently reconsidered (or perhaps decided to go back and tie bedsheets together) and tried to squirm back inside. But he was stuck.

Luckily, Javon was playing football in the parking lot below and noticed his neighbor losing his grip. "Let go, I'll catch you," the six-year-old reportedly shouted.

Brandon let go, missing a lower window ledge by inches, and fell safely into Javon's arms. A perfect catch and the crowd roared, "Javon, the hero."

In Baltimore, Maryland, two police officers responding to a fire also made a great catch when an infant's father was forced to toss him out a third-floor window.

Afraid that he would be unable to save his baby son, the father dropped the baby into the arms of Officers Richard Rutherford and John Walker.

Walker, who was quoted by *The Washington Post,* stated, "It was like trying to catch a touchdown pass. Don't drop this one. This is the one that counts."

While fire officials got the fire under control, Officer Rutherford climbed a ladder and brought down an eight-month-old baby.

Ground-Level Windows

It was a hot summer day and my six-year-old brother Greg, ten years my junior, was playing tag with a playmate in the backyard. Trying not to be tagged, Greg ran toward the sliding-glass patio doors, which were often kept open in the summer. The problem on this particular day was that someone had closed the doors. Greg crashed through the glass, suffering numerous cuts and almost severing a finger on his right hand. Bleeding profusely, he was rushed to the hospital.

Children do not fall out of ground-level windows and

glass doors, they run through them. In fact, at least 2,000 children each year are severely injured when they run, ride, or skateboard through ground-level glass doors.

The problem, of course, is that being glass, a closed door looks a lot like an open door. Probably seventy percent of these accidents would be prevented if parents affixed several strips of colored tape on the glass, at eye level for the child.

REDUCING THE RISK

- The greatest danger is the danger you never considered. "The danger of windows never even occurred to me," said one mother whose son broke his neck falling from a town-house window.

- Don't count on miracles or good catches. Install any of a wide variety of bars, window guards, or safety mechanisms that will either keep the window locked shut or prevent a child from falling out an open window. If you use bars, it is best to select a design that will keep young children in but will not prevent firefighters from gaining access. Remember, screens are not designed to prevent falls.

- Many communities now have laws that require apartment owners to install safety bars on windows if renters have small children. If your building does not have safety mechanisms on the windows, the owners may be in violation of the law.

- Statistically, beds that are next to or flush with open windows are particularly dangerous for children.

- Many children have fallen out of windows while trying to pull in clothes from a pulley-operated clothesline. Others have fallen out of windows while climbing on chairs or other furniture to reach something.

- Some young children have a difficult time distinguishing comic book and cartoon fantasy from reality. The children watch Peter Pan, Superboy, and other superheroes and believe they too can fly. One boy who fell out of a seventh-floor window had been flapping his arms and proclaiming, "I can fly, I can fly."

- Be especially careful when you remove window air conditioners; a window that was once blocked is now an intriguing gaping hole. Numerous falls have been reported from windows that previously contained air conditioners.

- Don't forget the obvious. Instruct children on the dangers of leaning out of windows or playing too close to open windows.

- Do not underestimate the ability of a toddler to open a window. If a screen and lock are your only safety features, make sure the lock is childproof.

- Most falls occur in the summer months when windows are open for breezes and children are leaning out of windows to observe neighborhood activities and to communicate with friends.

- In more than 2,000 recorded incidents children fell out of windows while leaning on loose screens.

- Adults who do not have young children often fail to consider the dangers of windows. When visiting people with high windows or balconies, remind them of the potential dangers. Children who live at ground level are often intrigued with the view when they visit a high-rise.

- Windows that are dangerous for children are also dangerous for pets. Sometimes referred to as the "high-rise cat syndrome" thousands of cats, dogs, and other pets plunge inexplicably from high-rise windows each year. Although one cat dropped forty-six stories and landed virtually unscathed, hundreds of pets die each year after falling out of windows.

6

Drowning Dangers: Pools, Bathtubs, and Buckets

Swimming Pools

In Virginia a seven-year-old girl drowned while playing with her three-year-old brother in a wading pool. The drowning at the children's home occurred after their mother, who had been watching them play in the tiny pool, went into the house for less than ten minutes. Authorities theorize that the girl slipped, hit her head on a deck railing, and drowned in a few inches of water. A two-year-old Florida boy drowned in a backyard swimming pool when his fourteen-year-old baby-sitter went to make a "quick call" to her boyfriend. The toddler was apparently trying to retrieve a toy floating in the pool when he fell in. In California a three-year-old boy drowned after riding his tricycle into the deep end of his family's swimming pool. The boy, who had learned to dog-paddle and stay afloat in a "drown-proofing" course, had been peddling his tricycle fifty feet from the swimming pool when his father left for a moment to talk with a neighbor. Seeing that the boy was missing, the father searched a number of other locations before thinking to look in the pool.

An average of 315 children under the age of seven drown in residential swimming pools every year in the United States. Another 2,500 children are treated in hospital emergency rooms for submersion accidents. Many of these near-drowning victims suffer permanent brain damage.

Sparkling and sensual, water has a magical quality that mesmerizes children and magnetically draws them closer.

Children have drowned in toilets, buckets, bathtubs, and even puddles on a rainy day. In Florida a seven-week-old boy sleeping in his crib drowned after the family's aquarium sprang a leak and water poured into his bed. A ten-year-old girl in Oregon drowned in a hot tub when her hair was sucked into an intake and she was trapped underwater. But eighty-five percent of the child drownings in the United States occur in swimming pools.

The most important lesson thousands of drownings have taught us is: *Never* take your eyes off a child when he/she is in or near any body of water, not even for a minute.

Drowning is a silent accident; you rarely hear a splash or a cry for help. Most drowning accidents occurred when an adult answered a telephone, went to the rest room, socialized with a neighbor for a short period of time, or briefly attended to some household chore like cooking or cleaning.

When more than one adult is present, there is often confusion as to who is responsible for the child. In many drownings reviewed by the author, one adult (parent, grandparent, or baby-sitter) thought that another adult was watching the child. "I thought my wife was watching William," said one grieving grandfather, "and she thought I was watching him." This confusion is especially prevalent during parties and large social gatherings.

In many cases the drowning victims were not being supervised by adults but by baby-sitters or older siblings under the age of nine. Being children themselves, these guardians were often easily distracted and too immature to grasp the importance of their duties or to handle an emergency situation appropriately.

In a review of nearly 1,000 drownings, almost fifty percent of the young victims entered or fell into the pool after leaving the house unseen. Children are miniature Houdinis and have an uncanny ability to unlock doors and escape the confines of cribs, playpens, porches, and playrooms.

With so many children drowning after wandering out of their homes, it is extremely important to install a barrier or fence around the pool in order to separate it from the house. The fence should be at least five feet high with vertical spacing of no more than four inches (so a child cannot squeeze through) and should not restrict a clear view of the pool. Naturally, the fence should be constructed so that it is difficult for a child to climb. The gate on the fence should be self-closing (adults often forget to close gates) and have a self-latching mechanism as close to the top of the gate as possible. If the latch cannot be placed near the top of the gate, it should be located on the inside or poolside of the gate so children will have trouble reaching it. Many pool owners install alarms on doors and gates leading to the pool so they will know if a child has penetrated a secure area.

It is also important that we become aware of the so-called "first time" phenomenon. After children drown, it is very common for parents to make comments like "that was the *first time* Johnny ever unlatched the gate" and "that was the *first time* Jennifer ever opened the screen door." Children learn new tricks and skills by the minute. A child who has always stayed behind a sliding-glass door will suddenly open that door and decide to explore the swimming pool. Just because a child has stayed in the house in the past does not mean he or she will do so in the future.

Flotation devices, such as plastic inner tubes and inflatable armbands, may provide parents and children with a false sense of security. There are several recorded cases in which children drowned even though they were wearing flotation devices. Another problem is that parents and baby-sitters are sometimes less attentive if the child is swimming with a flotation device. And in some cases the victims apparently forgot that the devices had been removed and, imitating the behavior of older swimmers, jumped into the deep end of the pool. Children under five often do not perceive the risks associated with water.

Parents may also be lulled into a false sense of security if their infant or toddler has taken swimming lessons and is able to swim a few strokes. Although swimming lessons are good, there is no such thing as "drown-proofing" a child. In a document called "Swimming Instruction for Infants" the American Academy of Pediatrics stated: "It may be possible to teach very young infants to swim and keep their heads above water, but it is questionable whether or not an infant can truly be taught water safety and proper reaction to an emergency." Even though preschoolers may learn to swim, it is important to understand that no young child can be considered "water-safe." Children, especially preschoolers, must be carefully supervised when in or around water.

Pool toys can also pose a problem. In dozens of cases, unsupervised children fell into swimming pools and drowned while trying to retrieve a ball or a toy. Some of the victims had played with the same toy in the bathtub and may have viewed the pool as just a larger version of the tub.

To a toddler, a floating chlorinator, fashionably camouflaged to look like an alligator or a swan, might be a tempting toy that he or she would like to touch.

Often described as perpetual motion machines, children are constantly exploring their environment and have the ability to disappear from sight very quickly. This ability is enhanced when the child is using a wheeled walker or a tricycle. Parents and baby-sitters should be advised that many drownings have occurred when children accidentally scooted or peddled into the pool. Drowning occurs in a very short period of time.

Drowning and near drownings are rarely the result of a single preventable action. When children drown it is usually the result of a sequence of events. Therefore, if we implement several layers of protection (supervision, education, barriers, locks, and so forth), we greatly reduce the chances that a single lapse in attention or one mistake will lead to a drowning.

Bathtubs

Most parents and baby-sitters are shocked to learn that hundreds of children left unattended for short periods of time have drowned in bathtubs. On March 23, 1994, in Severn, Maryland, a nineteen-month-old boy slipped under the water and drowned in a bathtub when his mother left him alone to answer a knock at the door. In Baltimore, Maryland, a four-year-old boy drowned in a bathtub on the second floor when his mother left him alone for twenty minutes while she vacuumed the first floor.

Tragically, bathtub drownings have been reported in every state. Most bathtub drowning victims are under the age of two, but scores of victims have been three, four, and five years old.

There is not always safety in numbers. In several cases two or more children were sharing a bathtub when one child slipped beneath the water and drowned. Typically, the surviving child or children were not old enough to recognize that the victim was in trouble.

Drowning is not the only safety issue; scores of children are scalded each year in bathtubs and some die from their burns. In Houston, Texas, an eighteen-month-old boy died in a bathtub of scalding water. The infant's mother put the boy in the bath about 5:30 P.M. and went into the kitchen to prepare supper. She returned about a half hour later and found the boy unconscious with severe burns on his entire body. Authorities were unsure how the water got so hot but the mother suspected that her son may have turned on the hot water faucet after she left.

In most bathtub scalding cases the parents or baby-sitters simply neglected to check the temperature of the water or forgot that children's skin is more sensitive to hot water.

Buckets

Dozens of children drown each year after falling into buckets that contain water or other liquids.

Five-gallon industrial buckets that are re-used for household chores pose the biggest risk for children between the ages of eight and fifteen months. Most children are somewhat top-heavy at those ages and the buckets are sturdy and don't tip over.

In Stamford, Connecticut, a ten-month-old boy drowned after falling into a five-gallon bucket filled with an ammonia cleaning solution. This case was similar to dozens of other bucket drownings. The child's mother was on the telephone briefly when the infant wandered off and somehow tripped into the bucket. She found him unconscious a short time later.

Since so many children have drowned in buckets, the Consumer Product Safety Commission is considering legislation that will require warning labels on five-gallon buckets. Another option being considered is to require certain performance standards so that buckets will tip over if a child falls in. Our best defense, however, is to be aware of the threat and to keep buckets away from young children.

REDUCING THE RISK

■ Most drownings occur during a momentary lapse in supervision. Never take your eyes off a child when he or she is in or near any body of water. When two adults are present, never just assume that the other adult is watching the child. Be especially careful during parties and other social gatherings; there are more children and more distractions. Alcohol and child care do not mix. Remember, *hundreds* of children have drowned when an adult answered a telephone, went to the bathroom, socialized with a neighbor, or attended to a household chore.

■ Make sure your swimming pool has a fence, barrier, or safety cover that guards against unsupervised access by young children. A fence should be at least five feet high with vertical spacing of no more than four inches. Fences should be designed so that they are difficult for children to climb.

■ Make sure doors and gates leading to your pool are self-closing and self-latching and are never propped open. Alarms will add an extra level of security. Latches should be out of reach of young children. You might want to add a sign that will remind swimmers and workers to keep the gate closed.

■ Remove toys and other floating objects when the pool is not being used. Children may see these toys and want to play with them.

■ Swimming lessons are very important but should not be relied upon as a substitute for effective barriers or constant supervision. There is no such thing as a "drown-proof" child.

■ Don't be lulled into a false sense of security simply because your child is wearing a flotation device.

- Make sure baby-sitters understand the dangers associated with swimming pools, bathtubs, and buckets. Does he or she know how to swim? Is your baby-sitter mature enough to handle the responsibility and duties of the job?

- All parents and baby-sitters should learn cardiopulmonary resuscitation (CPR).

- If a child is suddenly out of sight, check the swimming pool first.

- Make sure that baby-sitters and older children know where the telephone is located, know how to dial 911, and know your address. You might want to tape your address and phone number next to the telephone so that it is readily available.

- Be especially attentive if children are utilizing wheeled walkers, tricycles, or low riders in the area of a swimming pool.

- Never underestimate the ability of a child to open a locked door, crawl out of a playpen, or exit a home. Children are all miniature Houdinis and learn new tricks by the minute. Remember, when it comes to opening sliding-glass doors or unlatching a gate, there is always a first time.

- Hundreds of children nationwide have accidentally drowned in bathtubs. Never leave a child unsupervised while he or she is bathing. Always check the water temperature before placing a child in a bath. Parents should have everything needed—the washcloth, towel, change of clothes—in the bathroom before the baby is placed in the tub. Do not leave the child unattended while answering the telephone or the doorbell. Many parents purchase portable telephones that can be carried poolside or into the bathroom.

■ Buckets containing water or other liquids, such as cleaning solution, are extremely dangerous. Dozens of children drown in buckets each year. Statistically, the five-gallon industrial bucket poses the greatest risk. Be aware of the threat and keep these buckets away from children.

■ Remember, a curious child and unsupervised child can drown in any body of water. Between 1987 and 1995 at least twenty-five children drowned in toilets, fish aquariums and puddles.

Dog Attacks

On Christmas Day, five-year-old Billy Lowney of Manchester, New Hampshire, was probably wide-eyed with excitement when he spotted a large, fluffy, eight-month-old puppy chained in his neighbor's backyard. Clutching his favorite stuffed animals, little Billy wandered out of his family's unfenced backyard and approached Sasquatch, an eighty-pound Alaskan malamute. Within minutes Billy was dead. Sasquatch, who was considered docile and loving, clamped down on Billy's throat, severing a carotid artery and crushing bones in his fragile neck.

In Peoria, Illinois, six-year-old Amber Blair died after she was attacked in her own home by the family dog. About 8:30 P.M. Amber's father heard a loud growl from another room and, to his horror, discovered the dog—a German shepherd–collie mix—had Amber by the throat. Amber was rushed to the hospital but died from her wounds the next day.

Tyler Olsen, a blue-eyed, curly-haired sixteen-month-old boy from Little Egg Harbor, New Jersey, lost his right arm to a wolf–German shepherd hybrid. Attempting to pet the dog, Tyler reached through a chain-link fence in his baby-sitter's backyard and was immediately attacked. The baby-sitter attempted to pull Tyler free but the dog's powerful jaws tore off the toddler's arm. Surgeons were able to reattach the arm, but complications forced them to amputate it the next day. Tyler was one of three children in four months to lose a limb in dog attacks.

Step one in any safety or security program is to face up to the reality of the problem. The three cases just mentioned—and thousands of similar ones—are the reality.

More than 1.5 million children suffer canine bites each year in the United States. An average of twelve children, including toddlers and infants, are killed, hundreds are horribly mauled, and thousands require hospitalization for less serious bites every year.

Children are most frequently bitten by their own dogs or by a dog owned by a relative, neighbor, or baby-sitter. Only a very small percentage of victims are attacked by strays.

Typically, children are attacked when they climb a fence to retrieve a ball, when they take a shortcut through a private yard, when they surprise or attempt to pet a strange dog, and when dangerous dogs like pit bulls and Rottweilers are allowed to run free. Although domesticated, dogs are predatory animals, and are most dangerous when they are protecting their young or roaming in packs.

Infants and Toddlers

Tragically, many dogs react to infants—helpless and mewling—as wounded prey and instinctively attack. All 450 breeds of dogs have evolved from wolves and maintain certain instincts. Attack responses can be evoked when curious and clumsy toddlers step on paws, pull tails, disturb sleeping dogs, or innocently play with a dog's dinner dish. Since many canines instinctively discipline their own young with a quick, controlled bite, it is possible this same behavior is sometimes directed at human children, with more serious results. Dogs have learned to view adult humans as dominant wolves, feared and respected leaders of the pack. But human babies do not command the same respect. It is also suspected that dogs, like children, suffer a form of jealousy and are threatened when a new member of the family is brought into the home. In the wild, wolves will attack outsiders who threaten their turf. A child stares into a dog's eyes out of curiosity, but the animal may interpret this behavior as a challenge. And some dogs, like some humans, will attack without warning and without provocation.

Every year in the United States hundreds of infants and toddlers are killed or mauled by a wide variety of dogs. The harsh reality is that in every state there are cases in which babies have been dragged from their cribs, bitten in bassinets, pulled from high chairs, and even attacked in their mothers' arms.

In Fort Myers, Florida, a two-week-old girl was pulled from her crib and killed by her father's German shepherd. The child's parents put her to bed at 9:00 P.M. Two hours later they found her on the floor with 150 puncture wounds.

A two-month-old girl from Lansing, Illinois, was asleep on her grandmother's couch when Tiger, a pit bull–German shepherd combination, mauled her to death. The baby was being cared for by her grandmother while her parents celebrated their third wedding anniversary. The grandmother reported that she was sitting next to the sleeping child watching television when Tiger, the family pet, attacked for no apparent reason.

In hundreds of reported cases, dogs have bitten infants who were being held, breast-fed, changed, or lifted by their mothers. Many of the mothers reported that the dogs "had never done anything like this in the past."

Large and aggressive dogs, bred for fighting and protection, do not make the best pets for children. This is especially true if the dog has been mistreated or trained to attack, raised away from children, or killed another animal in the past. It can be a very dangerous sign when such a dog growls at an infant or stares at an infant without barking.

Existing data also illustrates that a tether does not guarantee safety; over 900 children are known to have been bitten, mauled, or killed by chained dogs. Sometimes children wander too close to a tethered dog and sometimes the restrained dog breaks free.

With dogs, as with people, past violence is the best predictor of future violence. If a dog has attacked children in the past, there is a very good chance it will attack children in the future.

If a dog has ever demonstrated aggressive tendencies, including aggression toward other animals, it should never be left unpenned or unleashed in the same room with an infant, even if adults are present.

The responsibility for keeping dogs at bay and infants and toddlers out of their reach rests with owners, parents, and baby-sitters. When children are attacked by dogs, it is often a situation in which the children were behaving like children, the dogs were behaving like dogs, and the adults (owners and parents) were behaving irresponsibly.

Dog Attacks Are Expensive

Having just returned from her ballet and tap lessons, seven-year-old Raynelle Tucker of District Heights, Maryland, joined three of her girlfriends in her great-aunt's backyard. With giggles and boundless energy, the girls were passing a ball to one another when it rolled into a neighbor's yard. As Raynelle chased after the ball, three Rottweilers and a mastiff squeezed under an unsecured fence and attacked her.

Hearing the horrible screams and the growls, neighbor Francis Crawford, fifty-eight, saved Raynelle's life when he came outside with his Yorkie–Chihuahua, Pinkey, and began to hit one of the dogs over the head with a shovel. Pinkey ran into the fray and jumped on one of the dogs coming at Mr. Crawford. All the dogs then turned on the heroic, but tiny, sixteen-year-old Yorkie–Chihuahua and killed him. Quoted in the *Washington Times*, Mr. Crawford stated, "My small dog jumped on one of those dogs to help me. That stopped the dogs from jumping me."

Raynelle was mauled. The dogs, each weighing over one hundred pounds, bit the dainty, sixty-eight-pound ballerina over one hundred times, breaking her collarbone, jaw, and rib, tearing chunks of flesh, and chewing through the nerves that control her facial expressions. With plastic surgery, physical therapy, counseling, and future operations, Raynelle's medical expenses alone could easily reach $250,000 . . . and her parents do not have health insurance.

Steven M. Cooper, an attorney representing Raynelle, said he was considering filing a lawsuit charging the county with negligence because police and animal control officials did not follow up on previous complaints concerning the dogs running loose. He also reported to the *Washington Times* that he might pursue a civil lawsuit against the dogs' owners. According to the laws of the county, dog owners are required to properly fence in or enclose all pets on their property. Mr. Cooper was quoted as saying that "an inexpensive clip could have closed the opening in the fence that the dogs crawled under before attacking Raynelle."

A review of over 1,000 dog attacks in the United States makes one thing perfectly clear: when an attack occurs, medical and legal expenses for dog owners and victims can be astronomical.

In 1993 the family of Tyler Olsen, the little boy whose right arm was ripped off by a wolf-dog hybrid, reached an $850,000 settlement. The Olsens sued the boy's babysitter, the owners of the hybrid wolf-dog, and the breeders of the animal. Since the attack, Tyler has required five operations on the arm, two operations on an eye, and suffered a stroke that left him with a limp in his left leg.

Other lawsuits resulting from dog attacks have recently been settled for $425,000, $800,000 and $2.6 million.

The wise parent faces up to the reality of the threat and takes precautions to reduce the risk. The wise dog owner does everything in his/her power to prevent an attack—and purchases liability insurance just in case.

Dangerous Breeds

Historically, pit bulls, Rottweilers, and wolf-dog hybrids have been responsible for the most serious attacks on children. Other breeds involved in fatal attacks against children include Dobermans, German shepherds, malamutes, and Siberian huskies.

The aggressive and unpredictable pit bull has been responsible for *thousands* of serious maulings worldwide and has earned the nickname "the Mean Breed." In Morgan, California, two-year-old James Soto wandered out of sight, and his father found him three minutes later pinned beneath a pit bull, still on its chain. James died from severe bites to the face and neck. Known for their incredibly powerful jaws, pit bulls have been bred for fighting for more than a century and are particularly dangerous because they often give no forewarning of an attack. Once considered the all-American dog—owners have included Teddy Roosevelt, Helen Keller, and James Thurber—pit bulls are increasingly being purchased by criminals to guard drugs and by macho owners who want the status of a four-legged weapon. As with every breed there are many happy pit bull owners who have never had any problems with their dogs. But there is no denying the facts: pit bulls have killed or horribly mauled people in all fifty states.

Rottweilers can certainly be "people" dogs and wonderful pets, but they too have been involved in hundreds of fatal and near-fatal attacks on children. In Saxonbury, Pennsylvania, two-year-old Steven Selfridge was bitten on every square inch of his body when he was mauled by six Rottweilers at his grandmother's home. Almost two years after the attack, Steven is still undergoing reconstructive surgery and skin transplants and still breathes through a trachea tube. In Kent, Washington, a sixteen-month-old girl was attacked and killed by a Rottweiler that her two-year-old brother had released from a pen in the family garage. The dog had previously been returned to its breeder by another family after it bit a small child and killed some chickens. Known for their thick jaws and muscular necks, Rottweilers can weigh up to 120 pounds. Because of their sheer size and energy, Rottweilers need extensive obedience work if they are going to be around children. Many of the Rottweilers involved in child maulings were raised away from people, crazed from being cooped up in cages and small apartments, and encouraged to be aggressive by their owners. A high percentage of the dangerous Rottweilers were involved in minor incidents (nipping at children, killing small animals, etc.) before killing or mauling a child, and a high percentage had a history of running loose, a fault of the owners.

Wolf-dogs, hybrids that are part wolf and part dog, tend to retain the instincts of wild animals and are considered by many to be undomesticable predators. They weigh up to 150 pounds, chew everything in sight, and are extremely difficult, if not impossible, to housebreak. Large and powerful, wolf-dogs are known for their ability to escape tethers and fences and have killed children in Michigan, Minnesota, Alaska, and other states. Wolf-dogs are even dangerous when they are caged. Toddlers in New Jersey, Montana, and Washington all lost arms when they tried to pet caged wolf-dogs. Instinctively, wolf-dogs will grab and pull anything that comes their way, whether it's food, a neighbor's poodle, or a child's arm. Wolf-dogs certainly do not belong in apartments or town houses. If kept at all, hybrids should be kept behind double security fences and given plenty of space to run. Although many owners will argue that wolf-dogs are just getting bad press, the data clearly illustrates that it is extremely dangerous for wolf-dog hybrids to be around children.

Any dog can be dangerous if it is mistreated, threatened, or selectively bred or trained for aggression. In fact, because of unwise breeding practices, there have been an increasing number of cases in which notoriously gentle golden retrievers and Labradors (the author's favorite breeds) have attacked children. These cases, however, are still very rare and are almost always the fault of irresponsible breeders and owners.

The Good News About Dogs

Skippy, a black and white beagle, was my best buddy throughout elementary school. Inseparable sidekicks, Skippy and I camped out in the same bedroom, played catch, explored any woods we could find, and antagonized Mr. Mean (as I called him) by sprinting across his lawn. Mr. Mean was fond of saying, "Next to kids I hate dogs." When I stole cookies, spilled grape juice on the carpet, or accidentally broke a lamp, I'd point to Skippy and say, "He did it." Skippy would bravely step forward and take the blame for his friend. On Sundays I'd tether Skippy to the outside of the church while I squirmed, sweated, and counted the seconds inside. Once he broke free and entered the church looking for me. Dodging four ushers with long-handled collection baskets, Skippy jumped onto the altar, loudly acknowledged the priest, and searched every pew until he found me. I tried to disown him, but the entire congregation laughed as

Skippy leapt, ears-a-flapping, into my lap. I was so embarrassed.

I've always felt a strong, almost spiritual kinship with dogs. When I was accused of liking dogs more than most people, I responded, "What's your point, of course that's true!" When a girlfriend gave me an ultimatum, "Either she [my dog] goes or I go," I woke up the next morning being kissed and snuggled by a doe-eyed, beautiful, blond . . . golden retriever. Long ago, I purchased a king-size bed to accommodate at least one large dog at my feet. And I immediately understood why Bob Stockman, my Marine Corps buddy, charged the machine-gun emplacement in Vietnam to save his German shepherd. He loved that dog. Bob "Don't-Shoot-at-My-Dog" Stockman, a Marine who read Kierkegaard and Camus on patrol, destroyed the enemy bunker, saved the dog, and won the Silver Star for bravery.

There are 50 million dogs in the United States and most interactions between pets and people are positive and healthy. Without question, more children are helped by dogs than are hurt.

Man and dog have been bonding together for 14,000 years. Address the safety issues and dogs will reward you with immense psychological, emotional, and even spiritual benefits. There are sled dogs, hunting dogs, and seeing-eye dogs. Dogs sniff out bombs and drugs for us and visit sick children in hospitals. Dogs protect us from criminals, wake us when there are fires, and provide us with unconditional and nonjudgmental love. Dogs are indeed man's best friend.

REDUCING THE RISK

- Face up to the reality of the threat. This year more than 1.8 million children will suffer canine bites. Twelve children will be killed by dogs this year, hundreds will be horribly mauled, and thousands will require hospitalization for less serious bites.

- Warn children that climbing fences and wandering through private yards can be dangerous if the owners have dogs. Tell children never to approach unfamiliar dogs. Children eating food should not wander too close to dogs.

- If dangerous dogs are consistently running loose, get involved. Notify the owners, the police, and animal control authorities and express your concerns. Follow up on your complaint.

- Infants and toddlers are especially at risk. Dangerous dogs should never be left unpenned or unleashed in the same room with an infant or toddler, even if adults are present. Remember, even a caged or tethered dog can be dangerous if the child wanders too close. Never ignore a sign of aggression.

- Always deal with a reputable breeder. Even gentle dogs like golden retrievers and Dalmatians can be vicious if improperly bred and trained.

- Large and aggressive dogs, bred and trained for protection, often make risky pets for children. This is especially true if the dog has been mistreated or trained to attack, raised away from children, or has a history of violence against people or smaller animals. Past violence is the best predictor of future violence.

■ Legal and medical expenses following a dog attack can be astronomical. Dog owners should carry $50,000 to $100,000 in liability insurance and post "Beware of Dog" signs if appropriate.

■ Proper training for dogs is very important. Train dogs early to accept authority and to avoid areas that are off-limits.

■ The responsibility for keeping dogs at bay and children out of their reach rests with owners, parents, and baby-sitters. When children are attacked by dogs it's often a situation in which children were behaving like children, the dogs were behaving like dogs, and the adults were behaving irresponsibly.

■ If you are threatened by a dog, stand still and try to remain calm. Dogs can literally smell fear. If the dog wants to sniff you, let it. In most cases, the dog will decide you are not a threat and go away. Don't scream, run, or turn your back on a menacing animal. If you say anything, speak calmly and firmly. Never stare back into a dog's eyes; the dog will view this as a challenge. If possible back away slowly from a menacing dog, and be aware of vehicles you could jump into, trees you could climb, or other avenues of escape. Look for sticks, tools, bicycles, or other objects that you might use as weapons. If a dog attacks, feed him your coat, purse, or anything else that might keep him occupied. If you fall or are knocked down, curl into a ball and protect your neck and head with your hands.

■ Remember, more children are helped by dogs than are hurt by dogs. Dogs protect us from criminals, wake us when there are fires, and provide unconditional love. Address the safety issues and dogs are indeed man's best friend.

8

Bicycle Safety

En route to the baseball field, nine-year-old Jason was furiously peddling his bicycle to the left of a long line of parked cars. Without warning, the driver of one parked car opened his door. Seven-year-old Mary Ann was coasting down the long hill in front of her apartment complex, blond hair blowing in the wind, when the strap to her book bag caught in the rear spokes. Frantically trying to keep up with the older boys, six year old "J.J." was practically standing on the peddles when his miniature mountain bike hit a pothole, a remnant of an unusually harsh winter. Jason, Mary Ann, and little "J.J." were three of the 500 children killed last year in bicycle accidents.

Representing freedom, independence, and adventure, bicycles, for most of us, are the ultimate symbol of a carefree childhood. With a hot wind blowing in our faces, a bicycle becomes a white stallion, a jet plane, or a race car wheeling us into a whole new world. We just jump on that bicycle and leave our worries far behind.

But a child's dream often becomes an adult's nightmare.

Each year, more than 500,000 bicycle-related injuries are treated in hospital emergency rooms nationwide. The accidents occur in suburban cul-de-sacs and on city streets.

Wear a Helmet

About 50,000 children in the United States suffer head and brain injuries in bicycle accidents each year. Wearing a helmet will reduce the risk of a head injury by eighty-five percent and will reduce the risk of a brain injury by eighty-eight percent. Bicycle helmets save lives!

It is important to choose a helmet that meets the bicycle helmet safety standards of the American National Standards Institute (ANSI) or the Snell Memorial Foundation (SNELL). Any helmet meeting these standards will be labeled. A good helmet has a hard outer shell to disperse impact and prevent penetration, and an inner liner of shock-absorbent material. Most helmets for children come with different-sized foam pads that can be inserted to make the helmet fit the shape of the child's head. Naturally, you do not want the helmet to slide forward and block the child's vision but you do want a helmet that protects the child's forehead. Good helmets may range in price from about $20 to almost $100—much cheaper than a funeral or a long stay in the hospital.

A helmet only works if it is worn. In the past, children

have resisted wearing helmets because they were for "nerds" and "dorks." Recognizing this resistance, designers and safety experts are beginning to change the image of helmets. Helmets are not as geeky as they used to be. In fact, helmets have become fashion statements as well as safety items. Feather-light and stylish, today's helmets are streamlined, wildly colored, and well ventilated. Some even have holes in the back for ponytails. Children love to decorate their helmets with stickers advertising their favorite theme or sports team. Adults are likely to wear helmets because they are cheaper than brain surgery. Children are more likely to wear helmets if they are convinced that it is fashionable or that "everybody wears one."

If your tough little tyke or your self-conscious adolescent still refuses to wear a helmet, here are some suggestions. First, wear a helmet yourself. Don't be like the father who puffs on a cigarette and tells his child that smoking is bad. Explain to children that soldiers wear helmets and that football, baseball, and hockey players wear helmets. Education is our best bet so share the statistics, share the reality. Explain that 500 children die each year in bicycle accidents and that thousands suffer head injuries that require hospitalization, surgery, and sometimes a lifetime of heartache. The reality is that thousands of children are in wheelchairs or worse because they did not wear helmets. Every one of these children would say, "Don't be stupid, wear a helmet!" Take your children to one of the many bike safety rallies. When they see large groups of people wearing helmets they begin to think that helmets are okay; helmets become peer-acceptable.

Most states are finally passing laws that make helmets mandatory. So when you are asked, "Why do I have to wear a helmet?" you can respond, "Because I love you and because it's the law."

REDUCING THE RISK

The following safety tips are relevant for all bicycle riders. Parents, encourage your children to follow these rules and set an example by following them yourselves.

- Always wear a helmet. Stay smart and beautiful, protects your brain and your head. Helmets save lives.

- Never wear headphones while riding a bike. You want to be able to hear the traffic around you.

- See and be seen. Wear clothes that make you more visible. If you ride at night, attach reflectors and lights to the front and rear of your bicycle. Wear reflective clothing or material, especially on your helmet, ankles, wrists, and back. Only ride in areas familiar to you. Brightly lighted streets are best. Always assume you are not being seen by a motorist. Young children should never ride at night.

- Stay alert. Watch for motorists opening parked car doors. Watch for potholes, railroad tracks, open manhole covers (you would be amazed how many bikes fall into manholes), and drainage grates. Be especially careful when the pavement is wet or icy. Use special care on bridges. Approach intersections with caution, as nearly seventy percent of car-bicycle accidents occur at intersections or driveways.

- Obey the rules of the road. Stop at stop signs and red lights. Signal your intentions and check all directions before making a turn. Ride on the right side in a straight and predictable path. Don't suddenly bolt left or right. Obey traffic laws.

- Check your equipment. At least twenty people have been killed after their front tires became disengaged. Make sure your brakes and tires are in good shape. If you are in an accident, check your bike over very carefully. If your bike has quick release wheels, it is your responsibility to make sure they are firmly closed at all times.

- Don't be a show-off. Hotdogging and reckless speed leads to hundreds of serious accidents each year. Don't ride double. Keep your hands and feet in contact with the bike. It is dangerous to ride barefooted.

- Do not ride a bike that is too big for you.

- Do not carry anything that hampers the control of your bike. Install rear baskets and racks. Front baskets have a dangerously high center of gravity and will hinder your balance and steering. Don't carry anything in your hands while riding.

- Make sure that straps, pant cuffs, shoestrings, and so on don't become entangled with the chain or the spokes.

- Baby seats (with babies attached) have been known to fall off moving bikes. Fasten baby seats securely.

The best seats have an enclosed section that protects the child's feet. Stirrups are dangerous because the child's feet can slip into the spokes. The child should always wear a helmet.

9

Dangerous Toys

Most people assume that if a toy is sold in a store, then it must be safe. This is a dangerous assumption. Each year, the United States government is forced to recall *millions* of toys because they are in violation of child safety standards.

An average of forty children are *known* to be killed each year because of dangerous toys. Thousands of other children are seriously hurt by toys each year and require hospitalization.

When buying toys there are many safety issues to consider. Choking continues to be the leading cause of toy-related deaths. Does a small toy pose a choking hazard? Does a large toy have small parts that might become detached and choke a child? A child might eat a toy if it looks like candy or food. Did you know that more children have suffocated on uninflated or broken balloons than any other type of toy? Does the toy have a long string, loop, ribbon, or cord that might strangle a child?

Many toys have hidden dangers. At least thirty-five

children are known to have been killed when the lids of their toy chests slammed down on their delicate necks.

Baby walkers, wheeled devices that allow young children to scoot from place to place, pose serious safety hazards and have drawn criticism nationwide. Thousands of children have been killed or injured when they accidentally scooted down stairs, into swimming pools, or into hot stoves. Walkers are no longer offered for sale in some states and are banned in some countries.

Toys may be so loud that they injure a child's hearing or they may have sharp points that could poke out an eye.

It is unknown how many children have been killed or mentally impaired because their toys, bedrooms, cribs, and art supplies contained high levels of lead, but the victims certainly number in the tens of thousands.

Exposure to lead is considered the most serious pollution problem facing children. Even low levels of lead exposure can cause developmental delays and intellectual impairment. High levels of lead can cause death. A 1990 law requires that children's crayons and art supplies be free of toxic material including lead, and all art supplies must indicate on the label whether they contain toxins. The Consumer Product Safety Commission (CPSC) recommends that parents should only buy crayons and art supplies that carry the label "Conforms to ASTM D-4236."

In April 1994 the CPSC recalled hundreds of thousands of boxes of crayons imported from China because they contained lead that could poison children. The recall order came after a Phoenix infant ate a crayon and suffered lead poisoning.

Only a tiny percentage of the crayons currently sold in the United States contain lead. But crayons, which apparently look delicious to thousands of children, are typically kept around homes and schools for years, often without labels or wrappers. Blood tests for lead should be part of routine health care for young children.

Protecting children from dangerous toys is the responsibility of everyone. Careful toy selection and proper supervision is the best way to protect children from toy-related injuries and death.

Choking Hazards

When the paramedics arrived at Teresa and Logan Lough's house, their two-year-old nephew, Zachary, was blue and was not breathing. Zachary, who died the next day, had swallowed a small plastic chicken.

"I handed him to a paramedic and that was the last time I was able to hold him," said Logan Lough when he testified before Congress. Like the parents and relatives of other choking victims, the Loughs were giving their support for legislation that would require labels on toys warning of the danger of choking.

During the last decade 187 children in the United States choked to death on toys. Hundreds of other choking victims were hospitalized but survived.

Any toy or any detachable part of a toy that will fit inside an empty toilet paper roll is considered a choking risk. Small eyes and noses removed from stuffed animals and dolls and removable squeakers on squeeze toys have been known to lodge in a child's windpipe. Children have swallowed and choked on a wide range of buttons, buckles, baubles, and bells that were pulled off larger toys. They have also choked to death on marbles, small balls, batteries, and plastic toys offered as prizes in bubble gum machines.

Balloons, when broken or uninflated, pose one of the greatest choking risks when children put them in their mouths. In fact, more children have suffocated on uninflated balloons and pieces of broken balloons than on any other type of toy. In addition, scores of children have suffocated while playing with plastic bags.

Infant rattles and teethers can also pose a serious choking risk. Rattles and teethers should be large enough so that they cannot enter and become lodged in an infant's throat. Both should be constructed so that they cannot separate into small pieces.

It is also dangerous to buy small toys that look, smell, or taste like fruits, candy, drink, or any other type of food. Thinking the toy is candy or something else to eat, a small child might try to swallow it.

Choking continues to be the leading cause of toy-related deaths.

Toy Chests

A thirteen-month-old boy was found dead with his head inside his toy chest and his neck over the edge. Trapped in this position by the fallen lid, the toddler died of asphyxiation.

Between January 1973 and January 1994 at least thirty-five children were killed when lids of toy chests fell on their heads or necks. Two other children suffered brain damage when lids hit their heads and hundreds of children have injured fingers and hands. Most victims are under two years of age.

The Consumer Product Safety Commission (CPSC) has done extensive and valuable research on the strangulation hazards of certain types of toy chests and other containers. The CPSC study pointed out that most toy chest accidents occur when children are reaching into the chest and the lid drops on their hands or traps them at the neck.

Another potentially fatal, but less frequent hazard is suffocation. In some cases children have climbed into toy chests to hide, sleep, or retrieve a toy. Since the toy chests were not adequately ventilated, the children suffocated when the lid slammed shut, locking them inside. Even if the children had the strength to open the lids, they were prevented from doing so because latches locked the lids shut.

CPSC recommends that the lid of any toy chest that is hinged have a lid support that will hold the lid open in any position to which it is raised. Toy chests should have ventilation holes. If the toy chest has a lid or a door, it should not have a latch that might lock and trap the child inside.

Video Games

Three men wearing black hoods burst into the bedroom of a young woman in a flimsy negligee. The men kidnap the scantily clad sorority sister and then hold her down while a fourth attacker plunges an electric drill into her neck.

This is one of the scenes from a very popular video game called *Night Trap.* Banned in Australia because it is too violent, over 100,000 copies of *Night Trap* have been sold in the United States. Impressionable children are watching that scene over and over again.

A $5-billion-a-year business, video games have become the nation's biggest selling toy. Unfortunately, almost seventy percent of these popular games promote violent, sexist, or sexually abusive themes. In a variety of video "games" like *Mortal Kombat* and *Lethal Enforcer,* people get hacked to death and blood splatters on the screen. In *Blades of Steel* you lose points if you *do not* get into a fight.

The new wave of video games feature live action characters that look like real people. With these interactive virtual reality videos, children do not just watch violence, they participate in it.

Although studies contradict each other on the impact of toys and games on young people, most parents and psychologists are convinced that violent video games promote antisocial and criminal behavior.

Bowing to public pressure, the toy industry has agreed to establish a rating system to help concerned parents weed out the most violent video games. However, the only way to determine if a video is appropriate for your child is to view the game before purchasing it. Don't buy blind.

REDUCING THE RISK

■ Choking continues to be the leading cause of toy-related deaths. Do not buy small toys or toys with detachable parts that might lodge in a child's windpipe. Toys that look, taste, or smell like food can be very dangerous. More children have suffocated on uninflated or broken balloons than any other type of toy. Plastic wrappings on toys should be discarded before they become deadly playthings. Rattles, squeeze toys, and teethers should be large enough so that they cannot enter and become lodged in an infant's throat. A pacifier should have a shield large enough so that it will not fit in a child's mouth. The shield should have ventilation holes so the baby can breathe just in case the shield does get into the mouth.

■ Toys with long strings or cords may choke or strangle a child. Never hang toys with long strings, cords, loops, or ribbons in cribs or playpens where children can become entangled. The Consumer Product Safety Commission (CPSC) recommends that crib toys have strings no longer than twelve inches. Remove crib gyms from the crib when the child can pull up on hands and knees; some children have been strangled to death by falling across crib gyms stretched across cribs. Never put a pacifier or other items on a string around a baby's neck. Remember too, children have strangled on coat and sweatshirt strings while using sliding boards and other recreational equipment.

■ Dangerous toy chests have killed thirty-five children. If a toy chest has a hinged lid, make sure it has a lid support that will hold the lid open in any position. To prevent the hazard of a falling lid, you may want to buy a toy chest with no lid, with a lightweight removable lid, or with sliding doors or panels. Make sure your toy chest has ventilation holes that are not blocked if the chest is placed against a wall. You do not want a latch that will lock the lid closed.

■ Toys with sharp points and edges or jagged broken toys can be very dangerous for young children. A toy sword and a plastic ax were both advertised as safe and soft but both badly cut a number of children.

■ Toy dart guns, archery sets, and several toys designed to be thrown have caused many serious injuries, especially to eyes. Rubber tips on darts and arrows frequently fall off or are removed by children. Avoid dart guns or other toys that might be capable of firing articles not intended for use in the toy, such as pencils or nails. Children should not be allowed to play with adult darts.

■ Our parents were right; BB guns do shoot out eyes! The author reviewed 288 cases in which children lost eyes to BB guns. In approximately thirty percent of the cases an older child accidentally shot a younger brother or sister in the eye.

■ Loud noises from cap guns and other noise makers can injure a child's hearing. Toy guns that fire caps must include the following label: "Warning: Do not fire closer than one foot to the ear. Do not use indoors." Make sure these warnings are adhered to by your children—warning labels alone do not ensure safety.

■ Keep baby walkers (wheeled devices that allow children to scoot from place to place), ride-on toys, and other wheeled vehicles away from stairs, pools, cars, and hot stoves. Baby walkers have been associated with thousands of injuries and have been criticized because they discourage children from learning to walk and they allow children to roll downstairs, out-of-doors, and into harmful objects. Use baby walkers only on smooth surfaces. Edges of carpets, throw rugs, or raised thresholds can cause a walker to tip over. Some cities have passed laws prohibiting the use of baby walkers by child-care providers.

- Become a label reader. Is your product "Flame Retardant/Flame Resistant"? Does the label say "Not recommended for children under three"? Does the label warn of the danger of choking? Does the label say "Washable/hygienic materials"? What is the content of lead in the paint? Look for quality design and sturdy construction.

- Exposure to lead is considered the most serious pollution problem facing children. Even low levels of lead exposure from paint or art supplies can cause developmental and intellectual impairment. Do not buy crayons and art materials unless they carry the label "Conforms to ASTM D-4236." When repainting toys, toy boxes, cribs, and children's bedrooms, avoid old paint that may be high in lead. Use new paint that conforms to the government lead standards.

- All toys are not for all children. Toys that are designed for older children should be kept away from younger children. Follow the advice on labels that give age recommendations. Some toys are fine for older children but may be hazardous in the hands of a younger child. Keep this in mind if you have children of different ages; younger children usually like to play with their older siblings' toys.

- Protecting children from dangerous toys is the responsibility of everyone. Careful toy selection and proper supervision is the best way to protect children from toy-related injuries and death.

About the Author

LOUIS R. MIZELL, JR., is an expert on criminal tactics, targets, and trends and has been featured on dozens of television and radio shows.

As a former Special Agent and Intelligence Officer with the U.S. Department of State, Mizell served in eighty-seven countries including such hot spots as Lebanon, Iran, Chile, Colombia, Peru, and the Philippines. In addition to his investigative and intelligence roles he was assigned to Secretary Vance's personal protection team; protected Senator Nancy Kassebaum in El Salvador; and worked at both the 1984 and 1988 Olympics.

Mizell also served in Vietnam with the U.S.M.C., has a master's degree in law enforcement from American University, and is author of two other best-selling Berkley books: *Street Sense for Women* and *Street Sense for Seniors.*

He has received over 1,000 invitations to speak on topics of terrorism and crime throughout the world and has taught a course on terrorism at American University. Mr. Mizell is currently president of Mizell and Company, International Security, a group in Bethesda, Maryland, that collects criminal and terrorist data on 4,000 topics.